EDUCATION, INC.
REVISED EDITION

EDUCATION, INC.
Turning Learning into a Business

REVISED EDITION

Edited by

Alfie Kohn
Patrick Shannon

HEINEMANN
Portsmouth, NH

Heinemann
A division of Reed Elsevier Inc.
361 Hanover Street
Portsmouth, NH 03801–3912
www.heinemann.com

Offices and agents throughout the world

The author and publisher wish to thank those who have generously given permission to reprint borrowed material:

"I Think Corporate" cartoon by Dan Wasserman. Copyright © Tribune Media Services, Inc. All rights reserved. Reprinted with permission.

Credit lines continue on page 181.

Library of Congress Cataloging-in-Publication Data
   Education, Inc., Revised Edition : turning learning into a business /
   edited by Alfie Kohn, Patrick Shannon.
      p. cm.
   Includes bibliographical references and index.
   ISBN 0-325-00489-7
    1. Education—United States—Marketing. 2. Commercialism in
schools—United States. 3. Industry and education—United States.
I. Kohn, Alfie. II. Shannon, Patrick, 1951–.

LB2847 .E39 2002
659.2′9371—dc 21

                                 2002005724

Editor: Lois Bridges
Production: Elizabeth Valway
Cover design: Lisa Fowler
Typesetter: Publishers' Design and Production Services, Inc.
Manufacturing: Steve Bernier

Printed in the United States of America on acid-free paper
06 05 04 03 02   VP   1 2 3 4 5

CONTENTS

EDUCATION, INC.
REVISED EDITION

Introduction:
THE 500-POUND GORILLA

ALFIE KOHN

> *The best reason to give a child a good school . . . is so that*
> *child will have a happy childhood, and not so that it will*
> *help IBM in competing with Sony. . . . There is something*
> *ethically embarrassing about resting a national agenda on*
> *the basis of sheer greed.*
>
> —Jonathan Kozol

I give a lot of speeches these days about the accountability fad that has been turning our schools into glorified test-prep centers. The question-and-answer sessions that follow these lectures can veer off into unexpected directions, but it is increasingly likely that someone will inquire about the darker forces behind this heavy-handed version of school reform. "Aren't giant corporations raking in profits from standardized testing?" a questioner will demand. "Doesn't it stand to reason that these companies engineered the reliance on testing in the first place?"

Indeed, there are enough suspicious connections to keep conspiracy theorists awake through the night. For example, Standard & Poors, the financial rating service, has lately been offering to evaluate and publish the performance, based largely on test scores, of every school district in a given state—a bit of number crunching that Michigan purchased for more than $10 million. Pennsylvania took the bait, too, and other states may soon follow. The explicit findings of these reports concern whether this district is doing better than that one. But the tacit message—the hidden curriculum, if you will—is that test scores are a useful and appropriate marker for school quality. Who has an incentive to convince people of that conclusion? Well, it turns out that Standard & Poors is owned by McGraw-Hill, one of the largest manufacturers of standardized tests.

With such pressure to look good by boosting their test results, low-scoring districts may feel compelled to purchase heavily scripted curriculum programs designed to raise scores—programs such as Open Court or Reading Mastery (and others in the Direct Instruction series). Where do those programs come from? By an astonishing coincidence, both are owned by McGraw-Hill. Of course, it doesn't hurt to have some influential policy makers on your side when it's time to make choices about curriculum and assessment. In April 2000, Charlotte K. Frank joined the state of New York's top education policy-making panel, the Board of Regents. If you need to reach Ms. Frank, try her office at McGraw-Hill, where she is a vice president. And we needn't even explore the chummy relationship between Mr. McGraw (the company's chairman) and George W. Bush (see "Reading Between the Lines" on p. 49). Nor will we investigate the strong statement of support for test-based accountability in a *Business Week* cover story about education published in March 2001. Care to guess what company owns *Business Week?*

Stumble across enough suspicious relationships like these and your eyebrows may never come down. However, we don't want to oversimplify. The sizable profits made by the CTB division of McGraw-Hill, as well as by Harcourt Educational Measurement, Riverside Publishing, Educational Testing Service (ETS), and NCS Pearson[1]—the five companies that develop and/or score virtually all the standardized tests to which students and prospective teachers are subjected—cannot completely explain why public officials, journalists, and others have come to rely so heavily on these exams. Let's face it: For a variety of reasons, people with no financial stake in the matter have become boosters of standardized testing.[2]

More important, even if one could point to a neat cause-and-effect relationship here, the role that business plays in education is not limited to the realm of testing. Indeed, its influence is even deeper, more complicated, and ultimately more disturbing than anything we might reveal in a game of connect the corporate dots. To begin with, schools (and children) have been turned into sources of profit in at least three ways. First, large corporations sell educational products, including tests, texts, and other curriculum materials. Second, many more corporations, peddling all sorts of products, have come to see schools as places to reach an enormous captive market, and they have done so by insinuating advertisements into the curriculum itself, and by paying off school districts so that they can advertise their brands in school buildings, on buses, and even in television commercials that students are compelled to watch. Third, some corporations make money by taking over the management of the schools themselves, or simply by owning schools outright as they would a car dealership or any other profit-oriented venture.

What those three methods share is their directness. Vivendi Universal, which owns Houghton Mifflin, which in turn owns Riverside, makes money selling textbooks or the Iowa Test of Basic Skills. Coca-Cola makes money by arranging to sell their brand of liquid candy, to the exclusion of all others, on school property. Edison, Inc. makes money (or will do so eventually, it assures its investors) by running whole schools. You'll find more information about each of these three strategies throughout this book. But you'll also find discussions about a more indirect way of turning learning into a business. When corporations can influence the nature of curriculum and the philosophy of education, then they have succeeded in doing something more profound, and possibly more enduring, than merely improving their results on this quarter's balance sheet.

This can happen when businesses succeed in creating "school-to-work" programs, by which children are defined as future workers and shaped to the specifications of their employers. It can happen when the whole notion of education as a public good is systematically undermined—an ideological shift that paves the way for privatizing schools. Finally, it can happen when a business ethos takes over education, with an emphasis on quantifiable results, standardized procedures to improve performance, order and discipline and obedience to authority. Students expect to be controlled with rewards and punishments, to be set against their peers in competitions, to be rated and evaluated by those who have more power than they do. None of this is particularly effective at preparing children to be critical thinkers, lifelong intellectual explorers, active participants in a democratic society—or even, for that matter, good friends or lovers or parents. But the process is exceedingly effective at preparing them for their life as corporate employees.

Rather ingeniously, some practices serve the interests of business in multiple ways simultaneously. For example, selling products in classrooms may immediately increase a company's market share but it also contributes to a socialization process whereby children come to see themselves as consumers, as people whose lives will be improved by buying more things.

Standardized testing may be an even better illustration in that it manages to achieve several goals at one stroke:

$ it brings in hundreds of millions of dollars a year to the handful of corporations that produce the tests, grade the tests, and supply materials to raise students' scores on the tests;

$ it screens and sorts students for the convenience of industry (and higher education);

$ it helps to foster acceptance of a corporate-style ideology, which comes to be seen as natural and even desirable, in which assessment is used less to support learning than to evaluate and compare people—and in which the education driven by that testing has a uniform, standardized feel to it; and finally

$ when many students perform poorly on these tests (an outcome that can be ensured from the outset, and then justified in the name of "raising the bar"), these results can be used to promote discontent with public education: "We are shocked—shocked!—to discover just how bad our schools are!" Again, this can create a more receptive climate for introducing vouchers, for-profit charter schools, and other private alternatives. (Anyone whose goal was to serve up our schools to the marketplace, where the point of reference is what maximizes profit rather than what benefits children, could hardly find a shrewder strategy than to insist on holding schools "accountable" by administering wave after wave of standardized tests.)

To the extent that colleges, too, are increasingly seen as ripe for a corporate makeover, testing younger students would make sense as part of a long-term strategy, as one instructor sees it from his vantage point in the university:

The whole standards movement, after all, is about restricting learning to what is *actually useful*: the memorization of information, the streamlining of knowledge to what can be evaluated by a standardized test. By curtailing the excessive autonomy of K–12 teachers and requiring them to teach "to the tests," we are preparing future college students for a brand of higher education designed and administered by the savviest segment of our society: for-profit corporations.[3]

There may be some sort of shadowy business conspiracy at work to turn schools into factories, but this seems unlikely if only because no such conspiracy is necessary to produce the desired results. Most politicians have uncritically accepted the goals and methods outlined by the private sector—and, with the possible exception of attitudes toward vouchers, there are few differences between the two major parties. Marveling that "Democrats and Republicans are saying rather similar things about education," a front-page story in the *New York Times* explained: "One reason there seems to be such a consensus on education is that the economic rationale for schooling has triumphed."[4]

More ominous is the extent to which even educators have internalized a business approach to schooling. Many of us defend "partnerships" between schools and businesses, willingly "align" our teaching to uniform state standards, shrug off objections to advertising in the schools, refer to learning as "work" or schooling itself as an "investment." The next time you leaf through one of the leading education periodicals—or listen to a speech at a conference—try counting all the different telltale signs of corporate ideology.

There's no need for executives in expensive suits to show up in schools: we're already doing their work for them.

* * *

Some readers may dismiss as rhetorical excess any comparison of schools with factories. In fact, though, the analogy was first proposed by people who were quite explicit about wanting to make the former more similar to the latter. Back in 1916, one Ellwood Cubberley wrote that "our schools are, in a sense, factories in which the raw products (children) are to be shaped and fashioned into products to meet the various demands of life."[5] In the 1950s, this way of thinking was still in favor. The writer(s) of a *Fortune* magazine article, "The Low Productivity of the Education Industry," informed readers that we should strive "to turn out students with the greatest possible efficiency . . . [and] minimize the input of man hours and capital. In this respect, the schools are no different from General Motors."[6]

The popularity of such parallels may wax and wane over time, but were Mr. Cubberley to find himself magically transported to the early twenty-first century, he would almost certainly feel right at home. He would immediately notice that thousands of American schools, some of them dating back to his own era are still open for, um, business, but literally resemble factories. Inside them, he would see, as Linda Darling-Hammond observed in 1997, that

> the short segmented tasks stressing speed and neatness that predominate in most schools, the emphasis on rules from the important to the trivial, and the obsession with bells, schedules, and time clocks are all dug deep into the ethos of late-nineteenth-century America, when students were being prepared to work in factories on predetermined tasks that would not require them to figure out what to do.[7]

Cubberley would likely be impressed as well by the remarkable power that business continues to have in shaping educational policy. Every few months, he would notice, another report on American schooling is released by a consortium of large corporations. These documents normally receive wide and approving press attention despite the fact that they all recycle the same set of buzzwords. Rather like a party game in which players create sentences by randomly selecting an adjective from one list, then a noun from another, these dispatches from the business world seem to consist mostly of different combinations of terms like "world-class," "competitive," and "measurable"; "standards," "results," and "accountability."

A few examples from the last decade that might set Mr. Cubberley's head to nodding: The Committee for Economic Development, consisting of executives from about 250 large companies, demands that school curricula be linked more closely to employers' skill requirements and calls for "performance-driven education," incentives, and a traditional "core disciplinary knowledge" version of instruction. Ditto for the Business Roundtable, which describes schooling as "competing in the education Olympics."

Besides endorsing narrow and very specific academic standards, punishment for schools that fall behind, and more testing, it approvingly cites the example of taking time in high school to familiarize students with personnel evaluations. The National Association of Manufacturers, meanwhile, insists on more testing as well as "a national system of skills standards designed by industry." And the Business Task Force on Student Standards says that "workplace performance requirements of industry and commerce must be integrated into subject-matter standards and learning environments."[8]

To scan these recommendations is to realize two things. First, most have been adopted as policy. To an extraordinary degree, business's wish becomes education's command. Second, they traffic in the realm not only of methods and metaphors, but of purposes and goals. The question is not just whether we will compare schools to factories, or even whether we will prescribe practices that will make schools more like factories. The question is what vision of schooling—and even of children—lies behind such suggestions. While a proper discussion of this issue lies outside the scope of this book,[9] it is immediately evident that seeing education as a means for bolstering our economic system (and the interests of the major players in that system) is very different from seeing education as a means for strengthening democracy, for promoting social justice, or simply for fostering the well-being and development of the students themselves.[10]

In the final analysis, the problem with letting business interests shape our country's educational agenda isn't just their lack of knowledge about the nuances of pedagogy. The problem is with their ultimate objectives. Corporations in our economic system exist to provide a financial return to the people who own them: they are in business to make a profit. As individuals, those who work in (or even run) these companies might have other goals too, when they turn their attention to public policy or education or anything else. But business *qua* business is concerned principally about its own bottom line. Thus, when business thinks about schools, its agenda is driven by what will maximize its profitability, not necessarily by what is in the best interest of students. Any overlap between those two goals would be purely accidental—and, in practice, turns out to be minimal. What maximizes corporate profits often does not benefit children, and vice versa. Qualities such as a love of learning for its own sake, a penchant for asking challenging questions, or a commitment to democratic participation in decision making would be seen as nice but irrelevant—or perhaps even as impediments to the efficient realization of corporate goals.

Some people in the business world object to this characterization, of course. They insist that modern corporations have similar goals to those of educators, that business today needs employees who are critical thinkers and problem solvers skilled at teamwork, and so forth. But if this were really true, we would see cutting-edge companies taking the lead in demanding a constructivist approach to instruction, where students' interests drive the curriculum—as well as a Whole Language model for teaching literacy. They would ask why we haven't thrown out the worksheets and the textbooks, the isolated skills and rote memorization. They would demand greater emphasis on cooperative learning and complain loudly about the practices that undermine collaboration (and ultimately quality)—practices like awards assemblies, spelling bees, and honor rolls, or norm-referenced tests. They would insist on heterogeneous, inclusive classrooms in place of programs that segregate and stratify and stigmatize. They would stop talking about "school choice" (meaning programs that treat education as a commodity for sale) and start talking about the importance of giving *students* more choice about what happens in their classrooms. They would publish reports on the importance of turning schools into caring communities where mutual problem solving replaces an emphasis on following directions.

The sad truth, of course, is that when business leaders do address these issues, their approach tends to be precisely the opposite: They write off innovative, progressive educational reforms as mere fads that distract us from raising test scores. This is evident not only from the reports sampled here (from the Business Roundtable and similar groups) but also from the consistent slant of articles about education that appear in business-oriented periodicals.

Moreover, while there may be more talk in boardrooms these days about teamwork, it is usually situated in the context of competitiveness—that is, working together so we can defeat another group of people working together. (Business groups commonly characterize students as competitors—as people who do, or will, or should, spend their lives trying to beat other people. Other nations are likewise depicted as rivals, such that to make our schools "world class" means not that we should cooperate with other countries and learn, but that we should compete against them and win.) While social skills are often listed as desirable attributes, business publications never seem to mention such qualities as generosity or compassion. While it is common to talk about the need for future employees who can think critically, there is reason to doubt that corporate executives want people with the critical skills to ask why they (the executives) just received multimillion-dollar stock option packages even as several thousand employees were thrown out of work. Corporations may, as we have seen, encourage high school English teachers to assign students the task of writing a sample personnel evaluation, but they seem less keen on inviting students to critically analyze whether such evaluations make sense, or who gets to evaluate whom. In short, what business wants from its workers—and, by extension, from our schools—in the twenty-first century may not be so different after all from what it wanted in the twentieth and even nineteenth centuries.

* * *

As must be obvious by now, this book makes no pretense of offering a "balanced" treatment of its subject, with an equal number of pro- and anti-business essays. Rather, as a collection of complementary critiques, it is itself meant to provide a small measure of balance, a tiny counterweight, to the overwhelming (and under-challenged) corporate point of view that surrounds us. In part because of their vast resources, the business community has no trouble disseminating its opinions on education. It doesn't take a degree in political science to figure out why politicians (and sometimes even educators) so often capitulate to business. For that matter, it isn't much of a mystery why a 500-pound gorilla is invited to sleep anywhere it wishes. But that doesn't make the practice any less dangerous.

Indeed, we might even go so far as to identify as one of the most crucial tasks in a democratic society the act of limiting the power that corporations have in determining what happens in, and to, our schools. Not long ago, as historian Joel Spring pointed out, you would have been branded a radical (or worse) for suggesting that our educational system is geared to meeting the needs of business. Today, corporations not only acknowledge that fact but freely complain when they think that schools aren't adequately meeting their needs. They are not shy about trying to make over the schools in their own image. It's up to the rest of us to firmly tell them to mind their own businesses.

NOTES

1. Notice that the phenomenon by which a company makes money by testing students, then turns around and sells the materials designed to prepare students for those tests, is not limited to McGraw-Hill. Many of the major textbook publishers are represented in this list of test manufacturers.

2. For other explanations, see Alfie Kohn, *The Case Against Standardized Testing* (Portsmouth, NH: Heinemann, 2000), esp. pp. 2–4; Robert L. Linn, "Assessments and Accountability," *Educational Researcher*, March 2000, esp. p. 4; and Gary Natriello and Aaron M. Pallas, "The Development and Impact of High-Stakes Testing," in *Raising Standards or Raising Barriers?*, edited by Gary Orfield and Mindy L. Kornhaber (New York: Century Foundation Press, 2001), esp. pp. 20–21.

3. Nick Bromell, "Summa Cum Avaritia," *Harper's*, February 2002, p. 76.

4. Ethan Bronner, "Better Schools Is Battle Cry for Fall Elections," *New York Times*, 20 September 1998, p. A32.

5. Elwood Cubberley, *Public School Administration* (Boston: Houghton Mifflin, 1916), p. 338.

6. The *Fortune* article is quoted in Daniel Tanner, "Manufacturing Problems and Selling Solutions," *Phi Delta Kappan*, November 2000, p. 198.

7. Linda Darling-Hammond, *The Right to Learn* (San Francisco: Jossey-Bass, 1997), p. 40.

8. Jeff Archer, "New School Role Seen Critical to Respond to Modern Economy," *Education Week*, 8 May 1996, pp. 1, 8; Catherine S. Manegold, "Study Says Schools Must Stress Academics," *New York Times*, 23 September 1994, p. A22; Business Roundtable, *A Business Leader's Guide to Setting Academic Standards* (Washington, DC: Business Roundtable, 1996); Mary Ann Zehr, "Manufacturers Endorse National Tests, Vouchers," *Education Week*, 14 January 1998, p. 14; Business Task Force on Student Standards, *The Challenge of Change:*

Standards to Make Education Work for All Our Children (Washington, DC: National Alliance of Business, 1995).

9. Many writers, of course, have grappled with education's ultimate goals. I attempt to sort through some of the underlying issues in *The Schools Our Children Deserve* (Boston: Houghton Mifflin, 1999), pp. 115–20.

10. See, for example, an analysis of the powerful Business Roundtable, whose "main objective is not quality education but the preservation of the competitiveness of corporate America in the global economy," in Bess Altwerger and Steven L. Strauss, "The Business Behind Testing," *Language Arts*, 79 (3): pp. 256–62 (quotation appears on p. 258).

I

COMMERCIALISM IN SCHOOLS

Let's connect the dots: Over here are corporations persuading public officials to reduce their tax obligations[1]; over there are schools so starved for resources that they must resort to selling advertising space to companies. Lower taxes *and* a new audience for their ads—this must be what businesses mean by a "win–win" situation.

Alex Molnar, author of *Giving Kids the Business*, opens our collection with a review of recent developments in the struggle over whether corporations should be allowed to infiltrate public schools. He quotes an executive who "can't see a downside" to having a school athletic conference named for his bank. Indeed, from a business perspective, you can understand the appeal of getting your name in front of that many eyes, and training young minds to remember and prefer your brand. But the downside appears as soon as we look beyond private profits and consider the practice of targeting children in schools from the perspective of public policy or simple morality.

That phrase, "targeting children in schools," appears in a report issued by the General Accounting Office—the research arm of the U.S. Congress—and that report is described in our second reading. Representative George Miller, who requested the investigation, talks about a "cold, calculat[ed] effort to make customers out of children," and the litany of examples in Constance Hays' article supports that conclusion: ads that flash on school computers, contracts ensuring the exclusive sale of one kind of soft drink, and so on.

Even more disturbing than having public schools sanction and expose children to advertisements is the fact that corporate propaganda is sometimes passed off as part of the curriculum. Math problems plug a particular brand of sneakers or candy; chemical companies distribute slick curriculum packages to ensure that environmental science will be taught with their slant.[2] A few years ago, someone sent me a large, colorful brochure aimed at educators that touts several free "school programs" helpfully supplied by Procter & Gamble. One kit helps fifth graders learn about personal hygiene by way of Old Spice aftershave and Secret deodorant; another promises a seventh-grade lesson on the "ten steps to self-esteem," complete with teacher's guide, video, and samples of Clearasil. It's worth thinking about how corporate sponsorship is likely to affect what is included—and not included—in these lessons. How likely is it that the makers of Clearasil would emphasize that how you feel about yourself should not primarily be a function of how you look?

Similarly, consider a hypothetical unit on nutrition underwritten by Kraft General Foods (or by McDonald's or Coca-Cola): Would you expect there to be any mention of the fact that the food you prepare yourself is likely to be more nutritious than processed products in boxes and jars and cans? Or that the best way to quench your thirst is actually to drink water? Or that a well-balanced diet requires little or no meat? Or that smoking causes cancer? (Kraft General Foods, and Nabisco, for that matter, are owned by a tobacco company.) No wonder John Olson, in his contribution to this section, suggests that the proper way to use corporate classroom materials is as examples of how propaganda works.

Finally, many schools have been unable to resist the offer of free televisions in exchange for making their students watch Channel One, a brief current-events program larded with commercials. This was the brainchild of Chris Whittle, a man whose expertise is not in education but in delivering potential consumers to advertisers. This particular project, where the potential consumers happen to be our children, is described in some detail by Russ Baker in the last article of this section. The news segment of Channel One broadcasts is unlikely to spur much useful discussion among students—in part because the program is often shown during a brief homeroom period in which there is no time for talking, only for passive viewing. But, then, the superficial news reporting really isn't the point: It's just an excuse for showing commercials, and these do have substantial impact. One study found that Channel One viewers (as contrasted with a comparison group of students) not only thought more highly of products advertised on the program but were more likely to agree with statements such as "money is everything," "a nice car is more important than school," "designer labels make a difference," and "I want what I see advertised."[3]

And they say kids aren't learning anything in school . . .

—Alfie Kohn

NOTES

1. The same corporations that complain about the inadequacies of our educational system are aggressive in searching for ways to avoid funding it. Former Senator Howard Metzenbaum had no trouble making this connection: "In speech after speech, it is our corporate CEOs who state that an educated, literate work force is the key to American competitiveness. They pontificate on the importance of education. They point out their magnanimous corporate contributions to education in one breath, and then they pull the tax base out from under local schools in the next. Businesses criticize the job our schools are doing and then proceed to nail down every tax break they can get, further eroding the school's ability to do the job" (quoted in Jay Taylor, "Desperate for Dollars," *American School Board Journal*, September 1992, p. 23). For more, see William Celis III, "Despite Touted Gifts, Business Tax Breaks Cost Schools Money," *New York Times*, 22 May 1991, pp. A1, A23.

2. "Your child's science teachers may be summering with Weyerhaeuser or the hunting lobby. They may be teaching about our food supply with a lesson plan developed and donated by Monsanto. And the video on how oil is formed? An Exxon production. . . . Andrew Hagelshaw, director of the Center for Commercial-Free Public Education in Oakland, said such programs are an attempt to establish brand loyalty. He said the logging companies and oil industry have figured out what fast-food restaurants have long known: 'If you just start educating people at young ages around these facts, then they accept it as truth,' and that means customers for life." (Chris Moran, "Education or Indoctrination?" *San Diego Union-Tribune*, May 13, 2002.)

3. Bradley S. Greenberg and Jeffrey E. Brand, "Channel One: But What About the Advertising?" *Educational Leadership*, December 1993/January 1994, pp. 56–58.

BUY ME! BUY ME!

ALEX MOLNAR AND JOSEPH A. REAVES

On June 18, 2001, the morning of their high school graduation in Haddonfield, New Jersey, Chris Barrett and Luke McCabe pulled on a pair of brightly colored T-shirts, climbed into a limousine, and sped off for New York City to pitch themselves on national television.

Chris and Luke appeared on the *Today* show on NBC to announce that they had become the first college students in the United States to be commercially sponsored. "We were looking at our dream schools and discovered prices were so high we couldn't afford it on our own," said Luke. "We'd have to find another way" (Keedle, 2001).

For nearly a year, the two ambitious high school seniors marketed themselves on their Web site [*www.chrisandluke.com*], unabashedly promising to do just about anything to serve as "spokesguys" for a corporation willing to come up with the money to send them to college. Luke announced he might be persuaded to get a tattoo with a corporate logo. He and Chris posed in front of bowls of breakfast cereal with a sign: "Sponsor us. We will eat your cereal even if we're not hungry!" And, in a move that epitomizes the continuing encroachment of commercialization in education, the two published a picture on the Internet of themselves with golf clubs beneath a caption: "Tiger has sponsors for playing golf. We need sponsors to go to college!" (Barrett & McCabe, 2001a).

Potential sponsors flocked to the duo. In the end, Chris and Luke signed an exclusive contract with First USA, a subsidiary of Bank One Corporation, the largest issuer of Visa credit cards in the world. First USA pledged to pay one year's tuition for each of the students with the possibility of extending the deal. The company also agreed to pay expenses for promotional activities. Chris enrolled at Pepperdine University, where tuition, room, and board for out-of-state students is $31,370. Luke chose the University of Southern California, where out-of-state tuition is $31,714 (Keedle, 2001).

Although careful to advocate financial responsibility in its promotion of Chris and Luke, First USA remains one of the world

17

leaders in issuing credit cards to college students, who often perceive plastic as easy money. Nellie Mae's recent analysis of student credit showed, for example, that one in three college students has four or more credit cards and that average credit card debt among students has soared nearly 50 percent from $1,879 to $2,748 since 1998 (Nellie Mae, 2001).

Chris and Luke's marriage to First USA was treated in the media and within marketing circles as a heartwarming example of the ingenuity and the entrepreneurial hustle that make the United States great. The morning after graduation, Chris and Luke did 30 consecutive interviews in five hours with television shows across the nation. They were featured in *USA Today* and *Teen Newsweek*. According to their publicists, the pair reached 50 million listeners, viewers, and readers during their first two days as "America's First Corporate-Sponsored College Students" (Barrett & McCabe, 2001b).

But for all the hoopla, Chris and Luke also became spokesguys for a darker side of the entrepreneurial spirit—the growing commercialism of schools and the conscious targeting of students to capture them as cradle-to-grave consumers. "We've gotten to the point where students don't mind being used," says Andrew Hagelshaw, executive director of the Center for Commercial-Free Public Education. "They don't see anything wrong with using themselves to advertise for their sponsors" (Zernike, 2001).

To gauge the public visibility, prevalence, and impact of different types of commercial activity in schools, the Center for the Analysis of Commercialism in Education has tracked and analyzed a steady rise in media citations of this subject from 1990 to 2001. Our recent review of reports on school commercialism—in the popular press and in education, business, and advertising literature—found, for the first time, declines in the overall number of annual citations but an increase in attention to certain key issues.

PROGRAM AND ACTIVITY SPONSORSHIPS

If universities follow the lead of a group of central Arizona high schools, the Big Ten someday could be known as the Boston Chicken Conference; Stanford could send its scholar–athletes to defend the Pac-Bell Championship instead of a PAC 10 crown.

"I can't see a downside to it," said Mike Kinnison, an executive of Wells Fargo, after his bank announced it paid $12,000 for naming rights to a new high school athletic conference in central Arizona. "The publicity alone, I don't know how much that would cost" (Roberts, 2001).

Corporations pay for or subsidize school events, activities, or scholarships in return for the right to associate their names with a good cause and to increase brand recognition in important market segments. Unfortunately, corporations also target classrooms, playgrounds, or athletic fields to tap captive, impressionable audiences.

In California, some high schools rich in athletic talent are known as "shoe schools" because Nike, Reebok, Adidas, and others give their products to students in hopes of courting future superstars. "The shoe companies are using the high school programs to increase their visibility, and that has created an uneven playing field," says Dean Crawley, a retired commissioner of the California Interscholastic Federation (Davidson & Spears, 2001). Athletic Director Jim Perry of La Quinta (California) High School says that shoes even play a role in school choice. "Open enrollment and shoe companies allow parents to shop their kids around for exposure and benefits, and that makes me sick" (Davidson & Spears, 2001).

EXCLUSIVE AGREEMENTS

In March, Coca-Cola announced it was backing away from the exclusive pouring rights contracts it pursued with schools during the past several years. The company said that it would allow competing drinks such as juice, water, and vitamin-rich products into school vending machines where it was a supplier. Coke executives also told the media that they were urging local bottlers to let schools limit sales of soft drinks at lunch and remove corporate branding from the fronts of vending machines (Toppo, 2001).

The change came after years of growing criticism about soft drink sales in schools. Two months before Coke's announcement, the U.S. Department of Agriculture (2001) criticized schools for sending mixed messages about nutrition by selling sodas and snacks on campus and asked Congress for authority to regulate food and beverage sales in schools. The request was a clear warning to

Coca-Cola and other soda producers and a response to studies showing that sodas have negative nutritional value and that as little as one can of soda a day contributes to teen obesity (Ross, 2001; Toppo, 2001).

Despite the much-publicized policy shift, Coca-Cola officials said this summer that they would continue to sign exclusive contracts if local school boards wanted them. More than a few school boards apparently did. In Maryland, school administrators and such organizations as the National Association of Secondary School Principals joined forces with local bottlers, vending machine lobbyists, and Channel One to defeat a bill aimed at limiting commercialism in Maryland public schools (Manning, 2001).

INCENTIVE PROGRAMS

Principal Jan Britz of Simi Valley (California) High School became a hit with her students last April when she waded into a tub of specially cooked noodle soup during an assembly and sang a rendition of the alternative pop hit "Pretty Fly (for a White Guy)" (Haight, 2001).

The stunt was one of several that a local radio station required southern California high school students to arrange to compete for an all-expenses paid prom at Six Flags Magic Mountain. Among other things, students had to write down every artist and band played on the station between 6 A.M. and 10 P.M. on a weekday and get on television holding a sign that included the names of the radio station, their school, a rock group, and two local disc jockeys.

Corporate incentive programs—especially for reading—have become part of the education landscape. One of the best known is Pizza Hut's Book It! program. Last year, former U.S. Education Secretary Richard Riley teamed with Pizza Hut representatives on a four-day back-to-school bus tour. The "Success Express" made stops in 15 cities promoting reading—and pizzas (Pizza Hut, 2000).

APPROPRIATION OF SPACE

Corporations are moving into school space by using school facilities for commercial activities and placing advertisements on rooftops, bulletin boards, walls, and in textbooks. Corporate sponsorships have paid for everything from $15,000 electronic scoreboards to seat cushions during the past year; the media produced more stories dealing with this issue than during the three previous years combined.

One area of concern was the increasing use of student-targeted publications by the entertainment industry to advertise violent R-rated films. The U.S. Federal Trade Commission (2000) criticized the entertainment industry for the practice in a follow-up study on the 1999 Columbine High school shootings ("Studios Should Not Sell Violence to Kids," 2000).

An emerging appropriation of school space occurs on schools' Web sites. Utah's Jordan Board of Education announced last April that it would place banner ads and links to Internet retail services on school Web sites. Board members said they hoped the "e-advertising" tactic would create "a cash cow for student programs" (E-Commerce Guidelines, 2001; Toomer, 2001).

Probably the most controversial appropriation of space last year was a program by Philip Morris to give away 13 million textbook covers. The brightly colored covers were distributed by Cover Concepts of Braintree, Massachusetts, and carried Philip Morris's name with a picture of a young snowboarder beneath the words: "Don't Wipe Out. Think. Don't Smoke." A history teacher in Mesa, Arizona, used the covers as part of his lesson on tobacco's role throughout U.S. history and asked students whether they knew about subliminal advertising. When several said the snowboard resembled a lighted cigarette, teacher Mike Evans helped his class organize a press conference that prompted Mesa school administrators to recall the covers (Spethmann, 2000). Similar controversies surrounded Philip Morris give-aways in other states, including California, Rhode Island, and Utah (Groves, 2000).

SPONSORSHIP OF EDUCATIONAL MATERIALS

Corporations and trade associations continue to supply schools with materials that purport to offer educational content. A prominent example from the past year was in Stockton, California, where several corporate sponsors teamed up to produce a 27-minute educational video entitled "Sally Says Your Manners Are Always Showing." Stockton's Food4Less grocery chain and Brower Durable Transmissions funded the video and an accompanying workbook, which featured the two businesses. Local Head Start classes and first graders in the Stockton and Lodi Unified School Districts received copies of the videos, and cable giant AT&T Broadband broadcast the program on local cable channels (Benston, 2000).

ELECTRONIC MARKETING

Channel One, the commercial television venture that pioneered electronic marketing, remains a leader in the field with access to 8 million teenagers in 12,000 elementary and high schools. In March, Channel One signed a multiyear programming deal with the National Basketball Association that allows it to cover all major events of the NBA and WNBA and to feature players from both leagues as cohosts on its programming (Shirkani, 2001).

Another commercial television venture, DirecTV, announced in May that it would give educational programming to up to 50,000 K–12 schools and fit 2,000 schools in low-income areas with the equipment needed to access the programming. Gina Magee, senior public relations manager for DirecTV, said that the company introduced the scheme for philanthropic reasons. Most of the 65 channels in DirecTV's school choice package, however, include advertising (DirecTV, 2001).

Leading electronic marketing efforts have been in the computer field, where corporations have provided equipment in return for rights to target students with advertising. Two key players, ZapMe! and N2H2, were dealt setbacks in 2000–2001. N2H2 agreed to remove banner advertisements from computers used by 47,000 students in Seattle after a citizens' movement criticized the practice (Ervin, 2001), while ZapMe! changed its name to rStar and announced it was getting out of the education business (Benner, 2001). Consumer advocate Ralph Nader once described ZapMe! as a "corporate predator" for bombarding school computers with advertisements and collecting online profiles of students (Ruskin, 1998).

PRIVATIZATION

Media attention to the management of public schools—especially charter schools—by private, for-profit corporations or other nonpublic entities has been intense during the past year, receiving more media citations than any other commercial activity in schools.

On May 2, 2001, Indiana became the 37th state, along with the District of Columbia, to pass a charter school law (Garrett, 2001). Charter school legislation often is the legal framework used by for-profit education management firms to conduct business. Since the first charter schools began operating eight years ago, 2,073 schools have opened, mostly in Arizona, Michigan, California, Florida, and Texas. The nation's largest for-profit education management corporation, Edison Schools, operates 113 charter schools with more than 57,000 students and is scheduled to take over another 17 schools in Las Vegas and Miami soon (Edison Schools, 2001b; Heins, 2001).

Edison, however, is under pressure. The San Francisco Board of Education conducted an investigation last spring into charges that Edison violated state education policy and discriminated against minority and special education students to inflate performance ratings. The board gave Edison 90 days to make improvements, then voted in June to sever its contract (Guthrie, 2001). Edison Charter Academy eventually was allowed to stay open under a new contract with the California Board of Education (Edison Schools, 2001c), but voters in New York dealt Edison another blow in March by rejecting the company's bid to take over five public schools (Chiles, 2001). Despite Edison's troubles, the company continues to expand. In June, a new school management company, LearnNow, merged with Edison (Edison Schools, 2001a).

A recurring point of contention about for-profit school firms is how to assess performance. Edison touted its academic success in a series of press releases last year. Critics, however, contended that those pronouncements were based on internal data framed to make Edison look good (Safer, 2001).

FUND-RAISING

School fund raising used to mean bake sales or car washes. These days, fund raising is big business. Students, parents, and members of the public routinely collect product labels or cash register receipts from particular stores to help raise money for school operations or extracurricular activities.

In upscale La Canada Flintridge, California, the latest fund-raiser was a black-tie ballroom gala packed with more than 600 donors that netted $200,000 for local public schools. But fund-raising often underscores inequity. In nearby Inglewood, California, an urban district filled with low-income students, PTA groups raised only about $60,000 all year (Fox, 2001).

FUTURE TRENDS

During the past year, the media have focused less attention on such commercial activities as corporate-sponsored programs and electronic marketing in the schools but more attention on privatization and appropriation of school space. Two possible explanations for these trends emerge.

One is that growing resistance to school commercialism is beginning to take effect. The citizens' movements that plagued Edison Schools and Philip Morris are signs of that resistance. So, too, were such legislative initiatives as the attempt to pass a bill to shield schools in Maryland from commercializing activities and the U.S. Department of Agriculture's efforts to convince Congress to impose greater control over nutrition in schools.

Another possible explanation is that schools are becoming so highly commercialized that corporate encroachments may no longer be news. When commercializing activities in schools become commonplace, those efforts tend to lose their news value. The norm is not news. Perhaps the trends reflect a little of both: inroads by opponents of commercialism and an acceptance of commercialism as the norm.

Of particular note again this year was the lack of voice in the education media on commercializing activity in schools. With the exception of a sharp increase in articles on appropriation of space in 2000–2001 and mild ongoing interest in the privatization issue, education journals have largely ignored school commercialism.

This year's report underscores the need for a serious, systematic look at the impact that commercialism is having on the nature of teaching and learning and on the ability of schools to achieve high levels of academic performance.

REFERENCES

Barrett, C., & L. McCabe. 2001a. "Wanted: Sponsors for Our College Education!" [Online]. Available: *www.chrisandluke.com/sponsor.html*.

————.2001b, June 26. "We Did It! We Are 'Sponsored' by First USA!" [Online]. Available: *www.chrisandluke.com/main.html*.

Benner, J. 2001, May 17. "Bill Takes on Ads at School." *Wired News* [Online]. Available: *www.wired.com/news/print/0,1294,43847,00.html*.

Benston, L. 2000, December 10. "Stockton, Calif: Company's Educational Materials Promote Corporate Sponsors." *The Record,* p. G1.

Chiles, N. 2001, April 3. Vote Against Edison was Overwhelming. *Newsday,* p. A14.

Davidson, J., & S. Spears. 2001, March 15. "Shoe-Company Influence Strong at High School Level." *Sacramento Bee,* p. C1.

DirecTV. 2001, May 21. "DirecTV Goes to School: Educational Partnership Helps Power California State Science Fair" [Press release]. Available: *www.directv.com*.

E-Commerce Guidelines. 2001, April 24. *The JSD Board of Education Newsletter* [Online]. Available: *www.jordan.k12.ut.us*.

Edison Schools. 2001a, June 4. "Edison Schools to Acquire LearnNow, Inc." [Press release]. Available: *http://biz.yahoo.com/pmews/010604/nymO56.html*.

————.2001b, June 28. "Edison Schools Reports Extraordinary Gains on Recent Tests at Several Sites Across the Country" [Press release].

————. 2001c, July 17. "Edison Wins Charter to Keep School Open." *San Francisco Chronicle,* p. A12.

Ervin, K. 2001, April 3. "Web Ads Removed from Computer Screens." *Seattle Times,* p. B3.

Federal Trade Commission. 2000, September. "Marketing Violent Entertainment to Children" [Online]. Available: *www.ftc.gov/reports/violence/vioreport.pdf*.

Fox, S. 2001, April 15. "Private Fund-Raising for Schools Runs Gamut." *Los Angeles Times,* p. B1.

Garrett, J. 2001, May 16. "Progress on School Choice in the States." *Heritage Foundation Backgrounder,* 143(8): 1.

Groves, M. 2000, December 7. "Critics Hit Philip Morris for School Book Jackets." *The Record* (Bergen County, NJ), p. A46.

Guthrie, J. 2001, June 29. "S.F. Schools Vote to End Edison Compact." *San Francisco Chronicle,* p. A1.

Haight, S. 2001, May 8. "Principal Uses Her Noodle to Help." *Ventura County Star* (CA), p. B1.

Heins, C. 2001, May 15. "Schools Inc.: Is Capitalism the Answer for Failing U.S. Schools?" *The Daily Yomiuri* (Tokyo), p. 18.

Keedle, J. 2001, June 19. "This College Education Is Brought to You By. . ." *Teen Newsweek* [Online]. Available: *www.msnbc.com/news/589518.asp.*

Manning, S. 2001, June 15. "The Littlest Coke Addicts; Soft Drinks in Schools." *The Nation,* 272 (25): 7.

Nellie Mae. 2001, February 13. "Study Shows Student Credit Card Debt Rising." [Press release]. Available: *www.pmewswire.com/gh/cnoc/comp/155295.html.*

Pizza Hut and Book It! 2000, August 16. Pizza Hut and Book It! Reading Program Sponsor U.S. Education Secretary Riley's Back-to-School Bus Tour." [Press release]. Available: *www.bookitprogram.com.*

Roberts, L. 2001, May 16. "N. Valley Schools Discover Rewards of Sports Marketing." *Arizona Republic,* p. 1.

Ross, E. 2001, February 16. "Soft Drinks Promote Obesity in Juveniles, Researchers Say." *Milwaukee Journal Sentinel,* p. 3A.

Ruskin, G. 1998, October 29. "ZapMe!: A New Corporate Predator in the Schools." *Commercial Alert* [Online]. Available: *www.commercial alert.org/zapme.html.*

Safer, M. 2001, May 27. "Gold in Them Thar Schools: Up and Coming Edison Schools Conjure Mixed Feelings." *CBS News Transcripts: 60 Minutes* [retrieved from Lexis-Nexis database].

Shirkani, K. D. 2001, March 28. "NBA Courts Channel One Teens." *Daily Variety,* p. 6.

Spethmann, B. 2000, December 1. "More Fuel to the Fire." *Promo* [Online; retrieved from Lexis-Nexis database].

"Studios Should Not Sell Violence to Kids." 2000, October 4. *Michigan Daily* (Ann Arbor, MI), p. 4A.

Toomer, J. 2001, March 23. "Schools Clicking in to Web Options." *Desert News,* p. B3.

Toppo, G. 2001, March 13. "Coke to Change How It Sells Soft Drinks in Schools." *Associated Press State and Local Wire* [Online; retrieved from Lexis-Nexis database].

U.S. Department of Agriculture. 2001, January 12. "Food Sold in Competition with USDA School Meal Programs: A Report to Congress." [Online]. Available: *www.fns.usda.gov/cnd/Lunch/CompetitveFoods/competitive.foods.report.to.congress.htm.*

Zernike, K. 2001, July 19. "And Now a Word from Their Cool College Sponsor." *New York Times,* p. A22.

NOTE

This article is a condensed version of the annual report on school commercializing trends by the Commercialism in Education Research Unit (formerly the Center for the Analysis of Commercialism in Education) at the Education Policy Studies Laboratory, Arizona State University. Sharon Lake of the University of Wisconsin, Milwaukee, provided research assistance. The complete report is available at *www.school commercialism.org.*

COMMERCIALISM IN U.S. SCHOOLS IS EXAMINED IN NEW REPORT

CONSTANCE L. HAYS

From exclusive soft-drink contracts to computers displaying continuous advertising, corporate marketing in public schools is rising sharply. But few states have laws in place to address the phenomenon, and most decisions on commercial arrangements in schools are made piecemeal by local officials, according to a report from the General Accounting Office . . . released [in September 2000].

"In-school marketing has become a growing industry," the report stated. "Some marketing professionals are increasingly targeting children in schools, companies are becoming known for their success in negotiating contracts between school districts and beverage companies, and both educators and corporate managers are attending conferences to learn how to increase revenue from in-school marketing for their schools and companies."

Until now, there has been no comprehensive effort to measure the number of commercial contracts with schools. But school board officials, consultants, and nonprofit organizations that follow education issues say it is clear that such contracts are far more common now than they were even two years ago.

About 25 percent of the nation's middle schools and high schools now show Channel One, a broadcast of news features and commercials, in their classrooms, and about 200 school districts have signed exclusive contracts with soft-drink companies to sell their beverages in schools. And in at least one case, students using computers in classrooms were offered incentives to enter personal data names, addresses, information on personal habits—which would then be sold to advertisers.

Recognizing that the nation's 47.2 million students are an increasingly lucrative target market for consumer product companies, school districts are often willing to join with corporations. They see the money as one way to supplement tight budgets without having to raise taxes. But at the same time, few school officials are an even match for experienced corporate marketers. "They're trained in the three R's, and the R's don't include retail," one North Carolina school official noted last year.

Over the last three years, many school districts have signed contracts with soft-drink giants like Coca-Cola and Pepsico, in which vending machines in hallways function as glowing billboards for their brands. A math textbook published in 1995 by McGraw-Hill and approved for use in about 15 states names many consumer products, including Gatorade, Sega and Sony video games and Nike sneakers, in its problems. McGraw-Hill said it received no compensation for the use of the corporate names.

Companies like ZapMe!, which is based in San Ramon, Calif., offer schools free computers with screens that include continuously flashing ads. ZapMe! also collects information that students provide and makes it available to its advertisers—including Microsoft and Toshiba, which also supply the computers—said Bob Stern, a spokesman for the company. [This program was abandoned in October 2000.]

The G.A.O. report cites textbook covers distributed by Clairol, Ralph Lauren, Reebok, and Philip Morris with company names and logos fully displayed. In New York City, the Board of Education is considering a plan that would provide computers for all of its students, starting in the fourth grade. The computers might carry ads and possibly encourage shopping on a particular Web site.

A spokesman for the National Soft Drink Association said local bottlers signed contracts with the schools in part to support the schools and in part to promote their products. "The brand loyalty that is gained by having these products available to kids when they get thirsty during the day is valuable to these companies," said Sean McBride, the spokesman.

All the activity has aroused concern in communities from Montclair, N.J., to Madison, Wis., to Birmingham, Ala., where companies have made deals with schools that let them promote their products to students. The demand for product placement in schools has even created a separate consulting niche.

School districts are expected to make decisions about commercial agreements using their own discretion, said Renee Williams Hockaday, a spokeswoman for the National School Boards Association in Alexandria, Va. "It is obviously a growing issue," she said, adding that the agreements "could be something positive, as long as the students don't turn into walking advertisements for these companies with no benefit to their learning environment."

The report, prepared over the last year, is the first government study to address commercialism in schools. It stops short of pinpointing the effects of in-school advertising, noting that "because advertising is ubiquitous in America, it is difficult—if not impossible—to distinguish between the effects of advertising to which students are exposed inside and outside of school." The G.A.O. will study the issue again in the next year or so and quantify the spread of commercial activity in schools.

The report, which includes color photographs of ads atop school bus stops, over computer carrels and on soda vending machines, was ordered by Representative George Miller, a Democrat from California, and Senator Christopher J. Dodd, a Democrat from Connecticut. In an interview, Mr. Miller said he was prompted by concern over data being collected about students through computers given to their schools by ZapMe!

"Not a lot of attention is being paid to whether parents agree with this or want their children to participate or not participate," he said. "Sometimes parents have a different opinion from that of the superintendent or the school board."

Senator Dodd said he planned to send letters to parent–teacher groups around the country to urge them to read the report. There is still time, he said, for lawmakers and others to resolve the issues. "This hasn't gotten totally out of hand yet," he said. "Most schools are still doing a pretty good job." He added, however, that he was shocked that many schools said they were unaware that the "free" computers they received from companies could be used to collect, and sell, marketing data from their students.

"There is a tremendous amount of information being solicited and used to market back to kids without administrative consent or parental consent," he said. "If you had an 8-year-old or a 10-year-old, would you allow someone to come into your house to do a survey on your child without your consent?"

The report is being hailed by some as proof that commercial activity in schools is a growing threat. "This is the first official government confirmation that commercialism in schools is a problematic issue," said Andrew Hagelshaw, director of the Center for Commercial-Free Public Education in Oakland, Calif., which has waged many grass-roots battles against soft-drink contracts and Channel One. "Public schools are publicly funded and are supposed to be the one place where kids don't get advertised to. It's completely inappropriate to turn that venue into a place where companies get to promote brand-name products."

Mr. Hagelshaw said he had seen something of a backlash against commercialism in schools recently. Last year, the 15-million-member Southern Baptist Convention passed a resolution against Channel One, because it advertises to schoolchildren. In Madison, Wis., one of the first school districts to sign an exclusive contract with Coca-Cola, the school board recently voted not to renew the arrangement. San Francisco earlier this year turned down an exclusive contract with Pepsi, Mr. Hagelshaw said.

Another longtime critic of commercial activity in schools predicted that the report would encourage state legislatures to act. "This is going to raise the visibility of this issue enormously," said Alex Molnar, a professor of education at the University of Wisconsin–Milwaukee, who directs the university's three-year-old Center for the Analysis of Commercialism in Education.

Mr. Miller and Mr. Dodd have sponsored a bill, now part of the Elementary and Secondary Education Act, that [was] pending before the House and would require parental consent for market-research activities in schools.

"Let's not pretend this is child's play," Mr. Miller said. "This is not some benevolent effort to give away computers. This is a cold, calculating effort to make customers out of children."

Mr. Molnar says students could be harmed by the promotion of products through schools. "One could argue that a person comes to the marketplace skeptical, as a consumer," he said, "but in a school, everything that's going on is supposed to be good for you. When you take that venue and you exploit it for a particular special interest, you do a lot of damage to children." For example, he added, soft drinks, candy, snack food and fast food are all advertised in schools in many places, lending them a credibility they may not deserve nutritionally.

"Ultimately, this is the kind of thing that promotes cynicism in children," he said.

DO NOT USE AS DIRECTED
Corporate Materials in the Schools

JOHN OLSON

The offer of corporate materials is one many schools cannot refuse. To begin with, corporations produce materials about up-to-the-second topics, using the latest advances in educational technologies—and everyone knows schools never have all the resources they require, especially current ones. In addition, not only are the materials free or available at low cost, but sophisticated training is often provided. Indeed, they are often linked—no training, no material.

Further, teacher groups and various state agencies may endorse corporate materials because they have participated in their development or share goals in common. Indeed, state agencies themselves are major sources of free materials, which naturally reflect the policies of government that the agency hopes to foster through the school system. These endorsing groups give the materials an aura of legitimacy, making it easier to use them, perhaps less critically than were they not endorsed.

Moreover, corporate materials themselves often have the look of bona fide educational ones. The packaging, the teacher guides, the handouts—all give the impression that the materials are part of the usual resources teachers use. Often corporate materials have this look because the contractors who work for corporations hire teachers to produce them.

It is not surprising that school boards cooperate with corporations in making materials available to schools. How can schools not use such materials?

Taking a critical look at any corporate materials—whether from government agencies or commercial corporations—is really a subset of critical analysis of text materials, and textbooks themselves are not exempt. It is quite possible to find slanted treatment in texts, treatment that is politically acceptable, but wrongheaded.

However, textbooks are written with intentions different from those of corporate propaganda. Educational virtues are supposed to, and generally do, control their production. But the corporation has a vested interest in the way you *think* about the subject matter of the materials. For example, the Milk Marketing Board cares how you think about milk—it has a partisan view about the benefits of milk. So does the Egg Marketing Board about eggs, as does McDonald's about how you view hamburgers. They want the public to think well of what they do. Conversely, educational textbooks are intended to get students to think critically and carefully about what they read.

Corporations are free, of course, to promote their views—we live in a plural society, and the marketplace of ideas is open for business. However, educators must be ever vigilant about the status of corporate materials: Why are they produced at all? What is their point of view? How should we think about the subject under study if we follow directions for their use? Why should we follow their directions at all? Intended as they are to rally people to a cause, materials produced with a public relations aim are prone to misrepresentation.

Clearly, schools need access to materials, but corporations cannot supply the materials we need. We can, however, use them as opportunities to learn about how propaganda works, to recover the deep messages of the materials. We can use them—but only cautiously. Teachers need access to other materials—books on nutrition, for example, from an alternative point of view. These other materials, alas, are not as well produced. They lack the input from official teacher groups, although they are often produced by teachers with alternative ideas. They receive neither corporate, nor government, nor official teacher support—only corporate materials receive such support, and many of these alternative materials are flawed. They, too, tend to hide key issues and distort the other side of things, but they do present an alternative view.

The only way any materials written with a propaganda intention—corporate, activist, or errant mainstream text—become educational is in the hands of teachers whose intention it is to engender critical awareness and independence of thought. This is the essential antidote to propaganda.

How can teachers engender critical awareness and independence of thought in their students? In the case of science, which is my particular area of concern, it is important for teachers to reflect on the way the subject itself is taught. Our very idea of what science is like as a discipline may be faulty as a result of how the subject is presented. Are we wedded to a static and antiquated idea of what the doing of science is like? Are we afraid of our ignorance of controversial issues? The first step in engendering the critical spirit is to take a critical view of issues and of how one's subject itself is taught.

Second, as texts often do not capture the spirit of critical inquiry, teachers must look elsewhere, seeking out groups with alternative points of view, for example, on energy, on nutrition, on health, and finding out the basis for their alternative view. We must analyze and evaluate what the text says about the way knowledge claims are dealt with, about competing theories in the subject, about how the subject is applied in everyday life, and about related social issues. An analysis of the deficiencies of texts gives teachers a platform for deciding what supplementary materials are needed and how they can be treated.

Third, teachers can supplement texts by designing their own materials. They could also form consortia for sharing their materials and for providing support to each other as they tackle the difficult task of introducing social issues in the classroom based on a critical approach to resources. This is not a new idea, but basing the development of such materials on a critical evaluation of texts and stressing social issues may be new for some, and so might be embracing a collaborative approach to such development.

In the end, it is the teacher who renders materials truly educational by making them serve educational purposes—the cultivation of critical awareness and independence of mind. Students need to be able to think for themselves, sort out the value basis of argument, see behind rhetoric, and assess the validity of the claims on their allegiance. These habits of mind run counter to the purposes of corporations whose very existence depends on uncritical allegiance to their products and their points of view. If corporations want to invest in materials directed at schools, that is their choice—they have a right to produce those materials. We have a responsibility to see them for what they are.

STEALTH TV

RUSS BAKER

At Clifton High School, a mostly white, working-class institution in suburban New Jersey, it's time for second period—and for Channel One, a public affairs TV broadcast available exclusively for school viewing. Mounted high in a corner of every classroom—as omnipresent an icon as the American flag—is a large-screen television set, provided by Channel One. The face on the screen is that of school principal William Cannici. Speaking into a microphone, he tries a few jokes, then announces student vocational-award winners. In Mrs. Rossi's Spanish class, restless students begin talking among themselves. Suddenly, the teacher shushes her charges: It's show time.

The hip-hop music starts. Heads bounce to the beat. Cut to two young, fashionably dressed anchorwomen, one white and one black. First up in the news is a tough sell to almost any viewership: the census. Point: Without an accurate count, schools can't get their rightful aid. The census form flashes on the screen. "Hey, I got that!" remarks a student. Channel One's reporter interviews a census spokesperson, a sexually ambiguous-looking woman with her hair pulled back in a ponytail. "What the heck is that?" a student in the back of the room asks with a chortle.

Time for a commercial break. Teens snowboard and dirtbike their way through the Mountain Dew life (170 calories, 46 grams of sugar per can): "Do the Dew!" Then a Twinkies spot (150 calories, 14 grams of sugar per two-pack).

Back to the news. As a story airs about the Pope's groundbreaking mea culpa over the Catholic Church's transgressions toward the Jews, much of the class is deep in chitchat; the teacher tries, without success, to silence the talk. Other students appear to be doing their homework. Two young women are checking their makeup, and four are resting their heads on their desks. Not one person has a comment about the story, described by *The New York Times* as "the most sweeping papal apology ever."

Another commercial break. As the first frames roll, a student shrieks, "Pokemon!" Declares another: "I need to get that!" Next

35

ad: "Join the Marines." One viewer chimes along with the script: "The Few. The Proud. . . ."

For 10 years now, the folks behind Channel One have been able to offer advertisers a dream demographic: a captive audience composed of nearly half of all American teenagers. (And they truly are captive, as Carlotta and D. J. Maurer, two students at Perrysburg Junior High School in Ohio, can attest. Their refusal to watch Channel One in school bought them a day in the Wood County Juvenile Detention Center.) On the condition that all teachers will air and all students will watch its daily satellite-broadcast programs, Channel One lends television sets and other equipment to schools. The company, which claims to reach a teen market 50 times larger than MTV's, profits by selling two of every 12 program minutes for commercials coupled with call-in contests and cool banter.

As noxious as these school-sanctioned ads are, Channel One's success is part of a larger trend toward in-school marketing: Textbook manufacturers insert proprietary brand names into math equations, corporations provide book covers emblazoned with their logos, soda companies entice school officials into signing deals for on-campus product exclusivity, and companies donate computers that have the ability, in some cases, to track the online behavior of individual students. A whole new industry of consultants has sprung up to help corporate clients position their products in schools.

Even in today's thoroughly commercialized environment, there is something especially insidious about school-endorsed product pushing. For one thing, schools are supposed to offer a haven from the worst the world has to offer. We authorize metal detectors and locker sweeps to prevent deadly violence on campus. But there are other dangers to impressionable minds. Channel One's hyperkinetic blend of "current-affairs broadcasting" and carefully targeted commercials blurs the line between fact and fiction, between reporting that at least tries to be objective and the self-serving rhetoric of the advertising business. Unquestionably, young people lack the media "literacy" skills necessary to understand fully what they are dealing with: A recent study cited in *Education Week* shows that ninth-graders who watched ads in which professional athletes endorsed products thought the athletes had themselves paid for the ads.

CHANNEL WHAT?

Few American adults have ever heard of Channel One—a remarkable fact, considering that one in four middle and high schools now broadcasts it and an estimated 40 percent of all high school students are compelled to watch its programming every single school day. Perhaps parents do not know about Channel One because their kids (some eight million of them, in 12,000 schools) do not tell them about it. As for the key American institutions—governmental, educational—that might be expected to raise an alarm, they have mostly been looking the other way.

[In the fall of 2000,] the first-ever government study of commercialization in the schools was published. The General Accounting Office (GAO) report, requested by two Democrats—Representative George Miller of California and Senator Christopher Dodd of Connecticut—notes that in-school marketing is dramatically on the rise and that deals between schools and companies are being made on a district-by-district basis. Local educators are not equipped to negotiate with crafty marketers bearing freebies, much less to address the larger educational issues. While the GAO study was being circulated, the Federal Trade Commission released a report specifically condemning the marketing of violent content to underage children.

In some ways, the "new" political interest in protecting our children from the onslaught of the marketers harks back to 1989, when Channel One was launched by entrepreneur Chris Whittle (later, in 1994, he sold the company to K-III Communications, now called Primedia). Initially, the service faced heavy criticism from liberal groups and from educational powerhouses such as the national Parent-Teacher Association, the American Federation of Teachers (AFT), the National Education Association (NEA), and various principals' associations; even the American Academy of Pediatrics frowned upon for-profit classroom television. But the well-financed company won over school system after school system, and effective opposition dried up.

Of late, none of the major teachers' or school administrators' organizations has seemed willing to mount a serious challenge to Channel One. Two years ago, NEA officials told Channel One critics that while the association remains opposed to the service, removing it from America's classrooms was not a priority. The AFT offered a similar line. And the National Association of School Principals rebuffed Channel One opponents several times when they requested a meeting. As a result, the battle against Channel One is being waged by several tiny public-interest groups and through scattered, small-scale parent uprisings. The educational establishment apparently believes that the issue lacks urgency.

Governmental bodies tend to accept the claim that the free equipment and the "news value" of Channel One more than make up for any downside; besides, the argument goes, local governments can address the matter if they so choose. Even the GAO report declares that it is impossible to differentiate the effects of bombardment by Channel One from those of the commercial messages directed at young people outside school hours. Although the GAO researchers were undoubtedly well-meaning, such a claim is a cop-out: Many in-school marketers specially design ads, promotions, contests, and the like to track the impact of their sales pitches.

Can anyone doubt that the ads on Channel One are grossly out of place in an academic environment? Mark Crispin Miller, a professor of media and culture at New York University who studied Channel One's content in 1997, concluded that its commercial messages reinforced bad body image, emphasized the importance of buying things, and glamorized boorish and loutish behavior. To ensure "stickiness," the ad campaigns often feature interactive components. One that I saw urged students to watch a film called *Never Been Kissed*, then to call in and answer questions about the movie's content in order to qualify for a chance to win a $500 shopping spree and a watch.

Rather than defend the indefensible, Channel One insists that the ads are not what matters. At the company's Madison Avenue headquarters, sleek, gunmetal-silver placards fit for the starship *Enterprise* proclaim "Education" and "Our Missions: To Inform and Empower Young People." These displays imply that the ads are a necessary evil that makes possible a bounty of fresh educational content and free equipment. Indeed, in a meeting with me last year, Channel One officials sought repeatedly to focus attention on the educational merits of their product. The company has been able to orchestrate favorable publicity ranging from a laudatory *New York Times* op-ed by a Catholic priest, who is also a principal in a Channel One school, to supportive statements from the ordinarily populist Senator Paul Wellstone of Minnesota.

Company executives claim that the broadcasts hold students' interest because they deliver important information in an appealing manner. (The students appear to identify with the youthful newscasters as stars; indeed, one of them, Lisa Ling, has moved on to anchoring a commercial-network morning show.) The solution to disaffection among youths, say executives, is to deliver a product that shows them how world affairs are relevant to them and their families. "We go to Kosovo and talk to kids who are their age," said Susan Tick, an outside PR representative for Channel One. "You don't connect with them otherwise."

Even by these standards, the compilation tape Channel One gave me was not impressive: It included a segment summarizing the Bill Clinton impeachment situation, delivered at a rapid-fire pace that seemed harder for an average teen to follow than a conventional news broadcast. The commentary is often self-promotional, with Channel One correspondents and anchors gushing about how they've gotten to travel to exotic places, and with interviewed students identified as attendees of "a Channel One school."

If we are to accept Channel One's request that it be judged on its news content, we have to face the fact that there just isn't much there. Of the 10 minutes of "news," only two to three minutes is breaking news, according to William Hoynes, a Vassar College sociologist who studies the intersection of media and education. The remainder is a hodgepodge of contests, self-promotion, light features and profiles, music intros, and pop quizzes. And Hoynes concludes that even those paltry hard-news minutes frame the issues in rigid terms that do not promote original thought or critical thinking.

Not surprisingly, Channel One doesn't offer any statistics to prove that its programs benefit students. "We have attitudinal studies showing that teachers believe it to be productive," said Jeffrey Ballabon, a Channel One executive vice president. "They know kids don't read newspapers. They also don't watch the evening news." Perhaps the citation of "attitudinal" evidence is necessitated by the findings of one study the company did commission: A 1994 University of Michigan analysis found that students performed just 5 percent better in high schools that aired the programs and 8 percent better in participating middle schools—and then only in an "exemplary" (read: highly atypical) environment in which the teacher actively sought to incorporate the broadcast content into the class and made sure the students were paying attention. There was no measurable increase in discussion of news outside the school or in efforts to seek out additional information from outside news sources.

Nevertheless, most administrators and teachers seem to love their Channel One. With good reason: The company provides TV sets and a broadcast system that the schools use for their own purposes, including the principal's morning addresses. "Our district is not a real wealthy district," explains Lawrence Westerfield, principal of Mt. Healthy South Middle School in Cincinnati, Ohio, which airs Channel One. "If you want the technology," says Westerfield, "you have to count on advertisers to pay."

Yet there is evidence that the schools aren't getting a very good deal. A 1998 study co-authored by Alex Molnar, an education professor at the University of Wisconsin–Milwaukee, concluded that broadcasting Channel One takes up six or seven days of instruction over the school year and costs American taxpayers $1.8 billion annually. Molnar, who heads the Center for Education Research, Analysis, and Innovation, compared the average cost of 12 daily minutes of a secondary school's time, or about $158,000 a year, with the total value of Channel One's equipment ($17,000) and the annual rental value of the equipment ($4,000). Even the value of the time spent watching the two minutes of commercials ($26,000) exceeded the value of the equipment. And those Channel One minutes add up. A child who views the shows from sixth grade to graduation will lose seven weeks of school time.

AD NAUSEAM

Despite Channel One's self-proclaimed educational mission, the company offers a different story to advertisers. As Channel One's then-president bragged to a youth marketing conference in 1994, "The biggest selling point to advertisers [is that] . . . we are forcing kids to watch two minutes of commercials. . . . The advertiser gets a group of kids who cannot go to the bathroom, who cannot change the station, who cannot listen to their mother yell in the background, who cannot be playing Nintendo, who cannot have their headsets on." Channel One continually conducts surveys about the spending patterns of teens; and its Web site, heavily touted on the shows themselves, provides an ideal means of obtaining direct feedback from the students.

Channel One also makes much of its public-service announcements, including those warning students to resist peer pressure to take drugs. Meanwhile, it airs ads stressing ways to be cool and brags to advertisers that controlled viewing in the classroom is the ideal way to play on teens' insecurity and desire to fit in.

Channel One makes a lot of money—$346 million in 1999 ad revenues—for its financially troubled parent company, Primedia, which reported a net loss of $120 million that year. With an estimated $200,000 price per 30-second ad (a rate comparable to the major networks'), Channel One is a crucial element in the company's future strategy. In its 1999 stockholder report, Primedia declared: "Our products serve highly specialized niches and capitalize on the growing trend toward targeted rather than mass information distribution. Many of the company's products, such as *Channel One News* . . . afford advertisers with an opportunity to directly reach niche market audiences. *Channel One News* has no direct competition in the schools but does compete for advertising dollars with other media aimed at teenagers."

With so vast a market at stake, Channel One has not been reluctant to spend in order to protect its franchise. When Republican Senator Richard Selby of Alabama, an ally of the ragtag band of Channel One opponents, initiated Senate hearings in 1999, Channel One dumped almost $1 million into a lobbying effort led by former Christian Coalition Director Ralph Reed and the powerful law firm of Preston, Gates, and Ellis—and effectively kept a lid on further action or hearings. Last spring a Shelby-sponsored sense-of-the-Senate resolution opposing commercialization of the schools was blocked by Republican Senator Sam Brownback of Kansas and heavy lobbying by Reed and former New York Senator

Alfonse D'Amato. The company has other means of winning support: Channel One's Ballabon insisted on faxing me a mound of positive letters; several from students mentioned free trips to Channel One's Los Angeles production studios.

Lined up against Channel One's PR juggernaut is a spirited and diverse coalition that includes Professor Molnar's group; Ralph Nader's D.C.-based Commercial Alert; the Center for Commercial-Free Public Education, located in Oakland, California; and Obligation, Inc., a group from Birmingham, Alabama, headed by Republican businessman Jim Metrock. When Metrock found out that his children were watching Channel One, he did his own study; he's been a committed opponent ever since. He has helped recruit a number of socially conservative groups—like Phyllis Schlafly's Eagle Forum and James Dobson's Focus on the Family—some of which are more concerned with what they perceive as risqué content than with commercialism per se. In addition, Channel One's critics convinced the 15.8-million-member Southern Baptist Convention to pass a resolution in 1999 opposing the enterprise.

That's about it on a national scale. Channel One likes to keep the battleground local, where school officials often lack the training and policy sophistication to ask tough questions about content control and educational philosophy. Thus far, only one state, New York, has banned Channel One from the public schools.

Still, a few small districts have voted to bar Channel One, and Metrock says that some teachers in schools contractually obligated to show the programs are nevertheless switching them off. The company has apparently responded by warning errant schools that it will yank its equipment. And Channel One has now retained Nielsen Media Research to measure student viewing in 1,500 schools.

Sooner or later, it seems, educational advocates are going to have to make Channel One and its ilk a priority. If we are really on the brink of a top-to-bottom reconstitution of American education, then surely the intrusion of corporate products must be addressed. And enthusiasm for these new methods of "improving" the educational experience bears scrutiny if the letters of support from teachers and principals that Channel One's Ballabon forwarded to me are any evidence. Many contained the sorts of appalling errors—in spelling, grammar, syntax, and exposition—that these educators are supposed to be helping students avoid.

Were the topic ever to reach the national agenda, many vexing questions about education itself would be raised. For example, Channel One advocates contend that the broadcasts make it easier to teach young people about the news because the young hosts know how to speak kids' language. This, of course, suggests that adult educators (and parents, for that matter) are incapable of discussing the ways of the world in a compelling manner—a sentiment not everyone shares. And anyway, in an America awash in exhortations to buy and consume, shouldn't institutions of learning and discussion be free from the constant pressures toward superficiality and conformity?

Meanwhile, Primedia has announced a merger with the Internet company About.com, which has intricate business partnerships with pornography purveyors. Conservatives are upset by that, as they are with Senator Brownback, who is a leader in denouncing violence in the media yet enthusiastically backs Channel One, with its advertising for violent movies.

This year opponents are likely to concentrate on challenging the federal government's role as a major Channel One benefactor through its paid advertising for the armed services and the Office of National Drug Control Policy. But if there's strong, broad, untapped sentiment against the juggernaut, it probably needs to coalesce fairly soon: Channel One officials told me the company looks forward to rolling out the programs in thousands of additional schools.

Kimberly Smith provided reporting assistance for this article.

II

TO MARKET, TO MARKET—MARKET LOGIC IN SCHOOLS

If the subject is automobiles—how they're manufactured and sold, and by whom, and in what quantity—we find ourselves in the realm of economics. But if we persist in relying on the models and methods of economics once the conversation has turned to, say, helping children learn, that is a very different matter. At the very least, it is worth questioning the tendency to transform the act of teaching, the material being taught, and even the people involved in the process into things that are bought and sold. This is part of a larger phenomenon—one psychologist calls it "economic imperialism"—in which nothing is exempt from the laws of the marketplace.

One very efficient way to turn learning into a commodity is by turning teaching into the process of preparing students to take standardized tests. The current testing mania is part of a "results-oriented and business-minded approach to public education," as Stephen Metcalf contends in this section's first reading: Those scores are education's bottom line. He proceeds to lay out the government–business connections that make that transformation possible—and very profitable to the corporations involved. Still other corporations, concentrating specifically on the market for test-prep materials, are aiming their products at elementary schools, as the second article, written by Karen Brandon for the *Chicago Sun-Times*, makes all too clear. Never mind Nike ads in the corridors: If you want to see economic imperialism at work, just watch Stanley Kaplan and Princeton Review slither into your child's school.

It's not only the methods we need to monitor, though; it's also the metaphors. A case in point is the tendency to talk about what students are doing in school as "work": class work, seatwork, homework, and so on. The baggage carried by this terminology is substantial, as I try to explain in the next selection, an essay originally published as a commentary in *Education Week*. To construe learning as working has profoundly disturbing implications, as does the practice of referring to the students themselves as "workers."

Pat Shannon, with whom I edited this anthology, weighs in with a short but pointed lesson in how the logic of the marketplace affects the way we teach reading and construe education itself. Bringing these issues down to the level of one little boy, he warns that children are "being asked to learn to read and write in particular ways because these ways are valued by business." With enough practice we will learn to pronounce "school to work" as if it were one word, and to forget about the purposes of education other than those related to preparing children to become employees.[1]

Regardless of their educational objectives, educators are finding it increasingly difficult to make sure there is enough money to go around. One result is the willingness to sell space on the walls (and computer screens) to the highest bidder. Another result is that teachers are placed in the position of having to raise funds on their own. Sara Freedman's monograph illuminates a topic discussed all too rarely: how teachers must market themselves by writing grants, and the effect of that process on everyone concerned. Some teachers are now defined by their ability to make money for the school as much as by their skill as educators. Even those who excel at the very specific skill of grant writing quickly find that they must "satisfy the 'agendas,' as they call them, of powerful private funding sources whose priorities . . . [may be] quite different from those that would be set by the individual school or classroom teacher," as Freedman explains. Moreover, the competitive system of grant-seeking ends up institutionalizing inequities in the educational system.

Of course, corporations have always seen schools as instruments for securing their own social and economic ends. We close this section with an excerpt from Samuel Bowles and Herbert Gintis' 1976 classic, *Schooling in Capitalist America*. These authors provide a broader context in which to understand the issues addressed by our other contributors. Schools, they observe, typically socialize children to obey authority, to expect to be controlled with rewards and punishments for persevering at tasks they are compelled to complete. This is precisely the mind-set that prepares students to take their place in our economic system—and thus to perpetuate rather than challenge that system.

—Alfie Kohn

NOTE

1. For a skeptical account of the real purposes, and the real beneficiaries, of certain school-to-work programs, see Hannah Finan Roditi, "Youth Apprenticeship: High Schools for Docile Workers," *The Nation*, March 16, 1992, pp. 340–43.

READING BETWEEN THE LINES

STEPHEN METCALF

On the morning of September 11, President Bush was sitting in the second-grade class of the Emma E. Booker Elementary School. The location is revealing: Up to the moment Chief of Staff Andrew Card whispered in his ear, Bush believed he was going to be an Education President. The second plane put an end to that, of course; and when he signed his education plan into law on January 8, the celebration was understandably muted.

Nonetheless, the legislation delivers a huge victory to Bush: This year's reauthorization of the Elementary and Secondary Education Act is widely regarded as the most ambitious federal overhaul of public schools since the 1960s. States will now test all students annually from third to eighth grade, while launching a federally guided drive for universal literacy among schoolchildren. Perhaps more strikingly, a political party that once called for the abolition of the Education Department has radically enhanced the federal presence in public schools. After repeating the mantra of local control and states' rights for a generation, the GOP now intrudes on both. What has happened?

The Bush revolution in education is the culmination of a decade of educational reform spearheaded by conservatives and business leaders. To gauge the significance of this trend, consider the original aspirations for an American public school system: As Horace Mann, and later John Dewey, saw it, public schools were necessary to fashion a common national culture out of a far-flung and often immigrant population, and to prepare young people to be reflective and critical citizens in a democratic society. The emphasis was on self-governance through self-respect; a sense of cultural ownership through participation; and ultimately, freedom from tyranny through rational deliberation.

Fast-forward to 2002: The new Bush testing regime emphasizes minimal competence along a narrow range of skills, with an eye toward satisfying the low end of the labor market. All this sits well with a business community whose first preoccupation is "global competitiveness": a community most comfortable thinking in terms of inputs (dollars spent on public schools) in relation to outputs (test scores). No one disputes that schools must inculcate the skills necessary for economic survival. But does it follow that the theory behind public schooling should be overwhelmingly economic? One of the reform movement's founding documents is *Reinventing Education: Entrepreneurship in America's Public Schools,* by Lou Gerstner, chairman of IBM. Gerstner describes schoolchildren as human capital, teachers as sellers in a marketplace and the public school system as a monopoly. Predictably, CEOs bring to education reform CEO rhetoric: stringent, intolerant of failure, even punitive—hence the word "sanction," as if some schools had been turning away weapons inspectors.

Nowhere has this orientation been more frank than in George W. Bush's policies, first as Texas governor and now as President. When he invited a group of "education leaders" to join him for his first day in the White House, the guest list was dominated by Fortune 500 CEOs. One, Harold McGraw, the publishing scion and current chairman of McGraw-Hill, summed up: "It's a great day for education, because we now have substantial alignment among all the key constituents—the public, the education community, business and political leaders—that results matter."

The phrase "results matter," like the popular buzzwords "accountability" and "standards," means one thing: more standardized testing. The Business Roundtable, an organization of powerful CEOs (including Gerstner) intensely focused on education issues, admits in one position paper that "voices of opposition to these policies . . . emanate from parents and teachers." No matter: Testing is a "bedrock principle" for the Roundtable, and the "leadership and credibility of the business community is needed" to make sure standardized testing becomes a reality.

Why the infatuation with testing? For its most conservative enthusiasts, testing makes sense as a lone solution to school failure because, they insist, adequate resources are already in place, and only the threat of exposure and censure is necessary for schools to succeed. Moreover, among those who style themselves "compassionate conservatives," education has become a sentimental and, all things considered, cheap way to talk about equalizing opportunity without committing to substantial income redistribution. Liberal faddishness, not chronic underfunding of poorer schools or child poverty itself, is blamed for underachievement:

"Child-centered" education, "progressive" education or "whole language"—each has been singled out as a social menace that can be vanquished only by applying a more rational, results-oriented and business-minded approach to public education.

And, not surprisingly, the Bush legislation has ardent supporters in the testing and textbook publishing industries. Only days after the 2000 election, an executive for publishing giant NCS Pearson addressed a Waldorf ballroom filled with Wall Street analysts. According to *Education Week*, the executive displayed a quote from President-elect Bush calling for state testing and school-by-school report cards, and announced, "This almost reads like our business plan." The bill has allotted $387 million to get states up to speed; the National Association of State Boards of Education estimates that properly funding the testing mandate could cost anywhere from $2.7 billion to $7 billion. The bottom line? "This promises to be a bonanza for the testing companies," says Monty Neill of FairTest, a Boston-based nonprofit. "Fifteen states now test in all the grades Bush wants. All the rest are going to have to increase the amount of testing they do." Testing was already big business: According to Peter Sacks, author of *Standardized Minds: The High Price of America's Testing Culture and What We Can Do to Change It*, between 1960 and 1989 sales of standardized tests to public schools more than doubled, while enrollment increased only 15 percent. Over the past five years alone, state testing expenditures have almost tripled, from $141 million to $390 million, according to Achieve Inc., a standards-movement group formed by governors and CEOs. Under the new legislation, as many as fifteen states might need to triple their testing budgets.

All of which has led to a feeding frenzy. Educational Testing Service, maker of the SAT, has always been nonprofit; but it recently created a for-profit, K–12 subsidiary—ETS K–12 Works—to provide "testing and measurement services to the nation's elementary and secondary schools." To help market it, the company replaced CEO Nancy Cole, an educator with a background in psychometrics, with an executive from the marketing wing of the pharmaceutical industry. As new CEO Kurt Landgraf recently declared, ETS has a "moral responsibility" to participate in the debate on the "viability of high-stakes outcome testing," for "the betterment of our society and the people in it."

The big educational testing companies have thus dispatched lobbyists to Capitol Hill. Bruce Hunter, who represents the American Association of School Administrators, says, "I've been lobbying on education issues since 1982, but the test publishers have been active at a level I've never seen before. At every hearing, every discussion, the big test publishers are always present with at least one lobbyist, sometimes more." Both standardized testing and textbook publishing are dominated by the so-called Big Three—McGraw-Hill, Houghton Mifflin and Harcourt General—all identified as "Bush stocks" by Wall Street analysts in the wake of the 2000 election.

While critics of the Bush Administration's energy policies have pointed repeatedly to its intimacy with the oil and gas industry—specifically the now-imploding Enron—few education critics have noted the Administration's cozy relationship with McGraw-Hill. At its heart lies the three-generation social mingling between the McGraw and Bush families. The McGraws are old Bush friends, dating back to the 1930s, when Joseph and Permelia Pryor Reed began to establish Jupiter Island, a barrier island off the coast of Florida, as a haven for the Northeast wealthy. The island's original roster of socialite vacationers reads like a who's who of American industry, finance, and government: the Meads, the Mellons, the Paysons, the Whitneys, the Lovetts, the Harrimans—and Prescott Bush and James McGraw Jr. The generations of the two families parallel each other closely in age: the patriarchs Prescott and James Jr., son George and nephew Harold Jr., and grandson George W. and grandnephew Harold III, who now runs the family publishing empire.

The amount of cross-pollination and mutual admiration between the Administration and that empire is striking: Harold McGraw Jr. sits on the national grant advisory and founding board of the Barbara Bush Foundation for Family Literacy. McGraw in turn received the highest literacy award from President Bush in the early 1990s, for his contributions to the cause of literacy. The McGraw Foundation awarded current Bush Education Secretary Rod Paige its highest educator's award while Paige was Houston's school chief; Paige, in turn, was the keynote speaker at McGraw-Hill's "government initiatives" conference last spring. Harold McGraw III was selected as a member of President George W. Bush's transition advisory team, along with McGraw-Hill board member Edward Rust Jr., the CEO of State Farm and an active member of the Business Roundtable on educational issues. An ex-chief of staff for Barbara Bush is returning to work for Laura Bush in the White House—after a stint with McGraw-Hill as a media relations executive. John Negroponte left his position as McGraw-Hill's executive vice president for global markets to become Bush's ambassador to the United Nations.

And over the years, Bush's education policies have been a considerable boon to the textbook publishing conglomerate. In the mid-1990s, then-Governor Bush became intensely focused on childhood literacy in Texas. For a period of roughly two years, most often at the invitation of the Governor, a small group of reading experts testified repeatedly about what would constitute a "scientifically valid" reading curriculum for Texas schoolchildren. As critics pointed out, a preponderance of the consultants were McGraw-Hill authors. "Like ants at a picnic," recalls Richard Allington, an education professor at the University of Florida. "They wrote statements of principles for the Texas Education Agency, advised on the development of the reading curriculum framework, helped shape the state board of education call for new reading textbooks. Not surprisingly, the 'research' was presented as supporting McGraw-Hill products." And not surprisingly, the company gained a dominant share in Texas' lucrative textbook marketplace. *Educational Marketer* dubbed McGraw-Hill's campaign in the state "masterful," identifying standards-based reform and the success of McGraw-Hill's "scientifically valid" phonics-based reading program as the source of the company's eventual triumph in Texas.

Is the pattern repeating itself at the national level? On the day he assumed the White House—the day he invited Harold McGraw III into his office—Bush called on Congress to help him eliminate the nation's "reading deficit" by implementing the "findings of years of scientific research on reading." Bush would loosen the purse strings on one condition: Instructional practices must be "scientifically based."

To the literacy cognoscenti, the meaning was clear: Classrooms must follow the conclusions of the National Reading Panel, a blue-ribbon panel assembled by Congress in the late 1990s to determine the "status of research-based knowledge, including the effective-ness of various approaches to teaching children to read." Thanks to the NRP report, the phrase "scientifically based reading instruc-tion" appears dozens of times in the new federal reading legislation. Education Secretary Paige recently explained in a speech before reading educators, "The National Reading Panel screened more than 100,000 studies of reading and . . . found that the most effec-tive course of reading instruction includes explicit and systematic instruction in phonemic awareness, [and] phonics."

Why is the same conservative constituency that loves testing even more moonstruck by phonics? For starters, phonics is tradi-tional and rote—the pupil begins by sounding out letters, then works through vocabulary drills, then short passages using the learned vocabulary. Furthermore, to teach phonics you need a textbook and usually a series of items—worksheets, tests, teacher's editions—that constitute an elaborate purchase for a school dis-trict and a profitable product line for a publisher. In addition, heavily scripted phonics programs are routinely marketed as com-pensation for bad teachers. (What's not mentioned is that they often repel, and even drive out, good teachers.) Finally, as Gerald Coles, author of *Reading Lessons: The Debate Over Literacy*, points out, "Phonics is a way of thinking about illiteracy that doesn't in-volve thinking about larger social injustices. To cure illiteracy, presumably all children need is a new set of textbooks."

Coles believes the NRP's conclusions, now implemented into law, are likely to be as friendly to McGraw-Hill's bottom line as Bush's policies were in Texas. "Combine the NRP report and the Bush legislation, and they suddenly have quite a paddle for rowing toward huge profits," he says. "Their products have been designed to embody the phrase 'scientifically based.'"

Several critics have emerged with key questions about the NRP report. To begin with, the 100,000 figure is wildly misleading. The central findings—those most likely to guide school practices, and thus their purchase of textbooks—involved only thirty-eight stud-ies. Coles argues that those studies are often themselves of ques-tionable relevance. On the decisive question of whether phonics instruction has an impact on reading comprehension, for example, the panel cited just three studies supporting a significant boost: one conducted in Spain, one in Finland and one comparing phonics to placing words and pictures into categories—as Coles puts it, in effect comparing phonics to "no instruction at all." Coles found the NRP report to be consistently slanted in favor of the skills-based, phonics approach. Another researcher, Stephen Krashen of the University of Southern California, complains that the report misrepresents his research and is rife with errors.

Nonetheless, the NRP report was sold to the public as a conclusive end to the so-called Reading Wars. It was presented to educators across the country, and reported by the media, as the triumph of disinterested science, largely by means of a thirty-page media-friendly summary and viewer-friendly video. Both are in lieu of a forbidding "Reports of the Subgroups," which weighs in at a media-repellent 600 pages.

Elaine Garan, an education professor at California State University, Fresno, has parsed through all three. She believes there are wide discrepancies between what was reported to the public and what the panel actually found. Most blatantly, the summary proclaimed that "systematic phonics instruction produces significant benefits for students in kindergarten through sixth grade," while the report itself said: "There were insufficient data to draw any conclusions about the effects of phonics instruction with normally developing readers above first grade."

According to one panel member, there is a simple explanation for the discrepancy: Widmeyer Communications, the powerful Washington, DC, public relations firm hired by the government to promote the panel's work. Widmeyer had represented McGraw-Hill's flagship literacy product Open Court during the Texas literacy drive, and now it counts McGraw-Hill and the Business Roundtable among its most prominent clients. "They wrote the introduction to the final report," says NRP member Joanne Yatvin. "And they wrote the summary, and prepared the video, and did the press releases."

Yatvin remains frustrated with Widmeyer's influence over the panel—from stacking public hearings with alumni from Bush's Texas literacy drive, to minimizing the impact of her dissent by burying her minority report. Yatvin even recalls, with disgust, a Widmeyer flack getting in between her and a reporter (Scott Widmeyer, Widmeyer's CEO, denies that this happened). Other panel members echo Yatvin's concerns, although the NRP chair, Donald

Langenberg, chancellor of the University System of Maryland, says the PR firm was "very nearly invisible" and insists the panel's reading recommendations were "balanced."

It has been phonics-based programs, however, that seem to have enjoyed a boost in the wake of the report. In Texas and California, McGraw-Hill literacy products have been adopted by school districts on the basis of their purported scientific validity. With the new education bill, Bush has tripled funding for early literacy, bumping it up to approximately $1 billion a year over the next six years. And he has just tapped Christopher Doherty to be in charge of spending that money. His qualifications? As head of the non-profit Baltimore Curriculum Project, Doherty brought DISTAR—McGraw-Hill's other literacy product—to Baltimore's public schools. "The bill stresses that the federal government must focus in early reading on those programs that have been scientifically proven to be effective," Doherty told the *Baltimore Sun*. "My job will be to help identify those districts and states that show they are going to implement K–3 reading programs based on that scientific research."

Phonics and testing, we're meant to believe, are an intensive therapy set to turn around laggard schools. But administrators, teachers, parents, and children know better; all are bracing for the changes wrought by the new legislation. In Oakland, the school board wants to spend its money somewhere else, introducing a resolution calling for the district to "cease immediately funding any and all identified un-funded state-mandated costs, including but not limited to state-mandated testing, assessment, and evaluations." Roy Romer, the superintendent in Los Angeles, told the *Pittsburgh Post-Gazette*, "It's a good bill only if they fund it." Apprised that the increase would come to roughly 35 cents per student per day, he concluded, "It's just a bunch of new mandates."

If this sounds like a dodge by those afraid of accountability, why the suspicion among successful districts? Last May more than two-thirds of eighth graders in the affluent New York suburb of Scarsdale boycotted a new standardized test, protesting the dumbing-down of the district's curriculum. Elizabeth Burmaster, recently elected Wisconsin's state superintendent of public instruction, finds the new legislation wasteful and redundant. "The money we have for public education is going to lowering class size," she says, pointing out that Wisconsin has worked hard to develop its own accountability system and that its students are perennially among the highest-scoring in the nation. "But the federal legislation basically says, 'Nope, you have to go back in and redo your state assessment system.' To what purpose?"

For the Bush Administration, passing the Education Bill may end up being the easy part. The public liked its emphasis on high expectations for schools and children (as opposed to the "soft bigotry of low expectations" attributed to bleeding-heart educators). A quasi-religious, and very American, faith in education helped the rhetoric of accountability to resonate; people half-consciously believe that schools ought to be able to equalize life opportunity, regardless of grinding poverty in one district, booming affluence in the next. But that disparity isn't going anywhere soon. The big players now at the education table, some with a considerable financial stake in the new regime, believe that money is best spent on testing and textbooks, rather than on introducing equity into the system over the long term. Meanwhile, thanks to a suave PR campaign, a large segment of the education community takes for granted that the science behind educational research is disinterested and rigorous. Both assumptions prevail in the current legislation; both need to be examined with clarity and skepticism in the years to come.

TEST-PREP PRESSURE HITS GRADE SCHOOLS

KAREN BRANDON

With 210 pages of practice exams and advice, the $12 work-book resembles the guides for students taking standardized tests for admission to college or graduate school. "Higher Score Guaranteed," the cover says. "Or your money back." But the students boning up for the test with this manual aren't applying to distinguished universities. They are trying to get to the 4th grade.

Students' promotion to the next grade, their entrance into elite educational tracks, the careers of educators, and the reputations and budgets of schools increasingly hinge on standardized tests.

When he took office last month, President Bush said his first order of business would be education reform. Bush said results would be measured "by testing every child every year," a point echoed by [Illinois] Gov. George Ryan in his State of the State address. New materials, tailor-made for nearly every test in every state at every grade level, are surfacing in traditional guidebooks, at tutoring centers, and through Internet-based services.

Though the multibillion-dollar industry has long sold test prepa-ration materials and services to schools, it is now trying to keep pace with the tremendous growth in tests given to elementary and secondary school students, and with the techniques made possible through technological advances. The industry increasingly is tar-geting parents directly in its drive to extend its reach to a younger clientele.

There is little agreement among educators about what is ap-propriate preparation for standardized tests. The new materials also raise basic questions: Are the children who improve their perfor-mance simply learning more about how to take tests? And are stu-dents whose parents or schools don't buy detailed test-preparation services at a disadvantage?

Publishers say they provide a needed service that helps students learn more, teaches them to do their best, and helps families and educators cope with mounting fear and pressure. Detractors say such materials prey on parents' and educators' anxieties and do not improve education.

California provides one of the most vivid examples of the test preparation debate. The workbook to prepare California 3rd graders for the state's standardized test is among the most detailed of a new genre of guides for elementary students, sold by Kaplan Publishing, a leader in the test-preparation industry: It is so detailed that it likely exceeds what the state allows in its classrooms.

Though California will distribute nearly $700 million to schools this year based exclusively on the results of one standardized test, the state's policy bars educators from using "any test-preparation materials or strategies developed for a specific test."

In Kaplan's view, California's ban on this kind of test-preparation highlights a gap Kaplan's materials fill. "While the motivation for this law may be to leave more classroom time for teaching important material and concepts, it has the effect of putting much of the responsibility for preparing for the tests on children and families." Therefore, "easy-to-use, clear and concise workbooks such as Kaplan's are essential," a company news release says.

"Guidebooks are only a minor part of the expansion of the $105 billion for-profit education business," said Peter Stokes, executive vice president of Eduventures.com, a Boston-based education research firm. Most of the growth has been in online tutoring aimed at schools and families. For instance, SmarterKids.com, an electronic educational store for children from birth to age 12, features a test-preparation center where parents can enter their child's test results. SmartPicks, the site's trademarked search engine, looks for "specific skill-building products for your child."

Kaplan says it is fostering a love of learning among the kindergarten through 10th-grade students whose parents buy into its educational services. But the names—Score! for the centers and eSCORE.com for the Web site—make its marketing strategy clear.

During the 1999–2000 school year, The Princeton Review, another leading test-preparation business, unveiled Homeroom.com. The program was initially tested in 25 Texas schools in grades 4 through 7. In November, the company announced results from five Houston schools, indicating that students who used the program showed greater improvement in math than students who did not. In the most extreme case, 6th graders who used the program showed a 4.5 percent improvement from the previous year, compared with a 1.6 percent decline in scores among students who did not.

The program has been sold to 130 schools, including three in the Chicago area, in almost a dozen states for an annual subscription fee of $4 to $7 per student per year, the company said. The Princeton Review declined to identify the schools. A company spokesman, who said he contacted the Chicago area schools, said school officials declined to be interviewed because it is "too preliminary" to discuss any results. This fall, the company plans to expand by offering subscriptions directly to parents and students.

Students using Homeroom.com take online sample tests that mimic standardized exams. They see their results immediately, and the program lets teachers, parents, and students know which areas need improvement. "We try to format and present the question as close to the form that will appear on the test as possible," said Stephen Kutno, vice president of educational policy and strategy for Homeroom.com. "[This] obviously is taking us into lower grades," he said, "but it is consistent with our view that test takers who are facing dire consequences really require an advocate, and we're that advocate."

Bush's proposal for yearly tests would mean most states would greatly expand testing, a survey by *Education Week* found. Nearly half of the states require or are about to require students to pass a test to get a high school diploma, and a handful of states are beginning to require children to pass tests for promotion to certain grades, the survey found.

Education Week concluded that the increased emphasis on testing has taken a toll. "State tests are overshadowing the standards they were designed to measure and could be encouraging undesirable practices in schools," it said. Marc Bernstein, president of Kaplan K–12 Learning Services, said the proliferation of high-stakes tests led the company to address the market in a way that is "very similar to the SAT preparation."

Ideally, Bernstein said, teachers would tailor the tests they give throughout the year to the style of the standardized tests children face in the spring. That is far better, he said, than "stopping your teaching four to six weeks before the test date and doing nothing but drill and practice, which is what a lot of schools do."

The skills students are learning with the company's tools are practical ones that apply to situations beyond the test, he said. "When you're facing a multiple-choice question, how do you eliminate some of the options that are given to you? To me, that's a lifetime skill in terms of the choices we make in our daily lives," he said. But Robert Schaeffer, public education director for FairTest, a Cambridge, Mass.-based organization that advocates testing reforms, disagreed. "These are short-term steroids to boost your testing power," he said. "People will do whatever they can to boost their scores by hook or by crook."

School districts pay for test-preparation materials at the expense of other items, he noted. Schaeffer expects the new menu of services will exacerbate the gap in performance of African-Americans and Hispanics, who tend to score lower than middle-class whites. Many parents and students welcome any assistance they can get. For instance, a New York parent gave five stars to the Kaplan guidebook for the state's 4th-grade test in a review on Amazon.com.

"This book really took all the mystery out of the New York State 4th grade testing. . . . I ordered more copies to distribute in my children's school." But a reviewer of a California guide said, "Nothing in this guide will improve the quality of the education the child receives." "The standards of what is acceptable in test preparation have changed in recent years," said Walter Haney, education professor at the Center for the Study of Testing, Evaluation and Educational Policy at Boston College.

"It used to be that most people would say that prepping kids on parallel forms of a test is inappropriate," Halley said. "But in fact it has come to be very widely accepted, so it's hard to condemn it. Many of the test companies themselves sell old versions of the tests." He characterized the advent of test-preparation books for the parents of young children as "an unfortunate reflection of the overemphasis on standardized testing." Drew Johnson, who wrote most of the Kaplan guidebooks with his wife, Cynthia, sees little harm in preparing for the tests.

"If you take the practice test, you're going to be familiar with the format," he said, "as opposed to just going in with your brain and a pencil and a willingness to do well. The books don't cause the anxiety," he said. "The anxiety is already there. What is an 8-year-old worried about? He's worried that if he doesn't pass this test, he might be held back or take summer school."

STUDENTS DON'T "WORK"—
THEY LEARN

ALFIE KOHN

September is a new beginning, a time for fresh starts. Consider, then, a resolution that you and your colleagues might make for this school year: From now on, we will stop referring to what students do in school as "work."

Importing the nomenclature of the workplace is something most of us do without thinking—which is in itself a good reason to reflect on the practice. Every time we talk about "homework" or "seat work" or "work habits," every time we describe the improvement in, or assessment of, a student's "work" in class, every time we urge children to "get to work" or even refer to "classroom management," we are using a metaphor with profound implications for the nature of schooling. In effect, we are equating what children do to figure things out with what adults do in offices and factories to earn money.

To be sure, there are parallels between workplaces and classrooms. In both settings, collaboration turns out to be more effective than pitting people against each other in a race to be No. 1. In both places, it makes sense to have people participate in making decisions about what they are doing rather than simply trying to control them. In both places, problems are more likely to be solved by rethinking the value of the tasks than by using artificial inducements to try to "motivate" people to do those tasks.

Even the most enlightened businesses, however, are still quite different from what schools are about—or ought to be about. Managers may commit themselves to continuous improvement and try to make their employees' jobs more fulfilling, but the bottom line is that they are still focused on—well, on the bottom line. The emphasis is on results, on turning out a product, on quantifying improvement on a fixed series of measures such as sales volume or return on investment. The extent to which this mentality has taken hold in discussions about education is the extent to which our schools are in trouble.

In the course of learning, students frequently produce things, such as essays and art projects and lab write-ups, whose quality can be assessed. But these artifacts are just so many byproducts of the act of making meaning. The process of learning is more important than the products that result. To use the language of "work"—or, worse, to adopt a business-style approach to school reform—is to reverse those priorities.

In a learning environment, teachers want to help students engage with what they are doing to promote deeper understanding. Students' interests may therefore help shape the curriculum, and a growing facility with words and numbers derives from the process of finding answers to their own questions. Skillful educators tap students' natural curiosity and desire to become competent. They provide information about the success of these explorations and help students become more proficient learners. Not every student relishes every aspect of every task, of course, but the act of learning is ideally its own reward.

Things are very different in a classroom where students are put to work, as Hermine H. Marshall at San Francisco State University has persuasively argued in a decade's worth of monographs devoted to the difference between work and learning environments. In the former, the tasks come to be seen as—indeed, are often explicitly presented as—means to an end. What counts is the number of right answers, although even this may be seen as just a prerequisite to snagging a good grade. In fact, the grade may be a means to making the honor roll, which, in turn, may lead to special privileges or rewards provided at school or at home. With each additional inducement, the original act of learning is further devalued.

It is interesting to notice how commonly the advocates of extrinsic rewards also endorse (a) a view of education as something necessarily unpleasant and (b) a curriculum that is in fact unappealing. A sour "take your medicine" traditionalism goes hand in hand with drill-and-skill lessons (some of which are aptly named "worksheets") and a reliance on incentives to induce students to do what they understandably have no interest in doing. Such is the legacy of seeing school as work.

"Measurable outcomes may be the least significant results of learning," as Linda McNeil of Rice University has observed, but measurable outcomes are the most significant results of work. Moreover, students are pressured to succeed because it is their "job" to do so; it is expected or demanded of them that they produce and perform.

It isn't hard to find schools that have undertaken this mission, where posters and bulletin boards exhort students to ever-greater success, which typically means higher standardized-test scores. (Many of these tests are normed, of course, so that success is defined as something that not everyone can achieve.) In such factory-like schools, you will often hear words like "performance" and "achievement," but rarely words like "discovery" or "exploration" or "curiosity."

Even those of us who do not recognize our own schools in this description may want to rethink the work metaphors that creep into our speech. We may wish to reconsider the extent to which learning is corrupted by talking about it as work—or by talking about learners as "workers," which amounts to the same thing. Even some progressive thinkers have given in to the latter temptation, intending to elevate the status of students but in fact compromising the integrity of what distinguishes classrooms from workplaces.

We are living in an age when education is described as an "investment," when school reform is justified by invoking the "need to be competitive in the 21st century." (Interestingly, Catherine Lewis, in her recent book *Educating Hearts and Minds*, reports that "the metaphor of the school as a factory or workplace where children do 'work,' so common in American schools, was notably absent from the Japanese [elementary] schools" she visited.) But if it is repugnant to regard children primarily as future workers—or, more broadly, as adults-in-the-making—it is worse to see what children do right now as work.

To get a sense of whether students view themselves as workers or as learners, we need only ask them (during class) what they are doing. "I'm doing my work" is one possible response; "I'm trying to figure out why the character in this story told her friend to go away" is something else altogether. Better yet, we might ask students *why* they are doing something, and then attend to the difference between "Because Ms. Taylor told us to" or "It's going to be on the test," on the one hand, and "Because I just don't get why this character would say that!" on the other.

Another way to judge the orientation of a classroom is to watch for the teacher's reaction to mistakes. Someone who manages students' work is likely to strive for zero defects: perfect papers and assignments that receive the maximum number of points. Someone who facilitates students' learning welcomes mistakes—first, because they are invaluable clues as to how the student is thinking, and second, because to do so creates a climate of safety that ultimately promotes more successful learning.

Moreover, a learning-oriented classroom is more likely to be characterized by the thoughtful exploration of complicated issues than by a curriculum based on memorizing right answers. As Hermine Marshall has observed, for students to see themselves as learning, "the tasks provided must be those that require higher-order thinking skills."

Does a rejection of the models, methods, and metaphors of work mean that school should be about play? In a word, no. False dichotomies are popular because they make choosing easy, and the "work vs. play" polarity is a case in point. Learning is a third alternative, where the primary purpose is neither play-like enjoyment (although the process can be deeply satisfying) nor the work-like completion of error-free products (although the process can involve intense effort and concentration).

To challenge the work metaphor is not to abandon rigor or excellence. Rather, it is to insist that work is not the only activity that can be pursued rigorously—and play, for that matter, is not the only activity that can be experienced as pleasurable.

Of course, to talk about students' "projects" or "activities" instead of their "work" represents only a change in language. My objective here is not to add to the list of words we are not supposed to mention. But how we speak not only reflects the way we think; it contributes to it as well. Perhaps a thoughtful discussion about the hidden implications of workplace metaphors will invite us to consider changing what we do as well as what we say.

WE CAN WORK IT OUT

PATRICK SHANNON

Jeffery Peter Malcolm was assigned an essay to write at home on what he wanted to be when he grew up. At age 8, his mind wandered across several fields—firefighter, rock star, engineer (like his mother), or art editor (like his father). I learned about Jeffery's assignment and aspirations when his mother called to ask for help with his writing development. Jeffery's father and I play basketball together in a lunch-time league. She reported that Jeffery seemed lost in terms of organizing his thoughts, in translating those thoughts into complete sentences, and in recording those sentences on paper. Her basic concern was the hopeless look on his face as he confessed his confusion.

His mother wanted me to understand that Jeffery was doing well in math and science and that he could explain the workings of the motor that ran his scooter. After a few questions, she confided that Jeffery's choices among occupations were a giant step forward because at age 6, when his teacher last asked this question, he replied that he wanted to grow up to be Super Mario. (I'm not certain whether he wanted to be Mario or the video game itself, and I didn't ask.) I discovered later that this assignment was part of his school's career awareness curriculum.

CAREER AWARENESS ACTIVITIES

According to the glossary of terms from the National School-to-Work Office, career awareness activities are "designed to make students aware of the broad range of careers and/or occupations in the world of work, including options that may not be traditional for their gender, race, or ethnicity." Jeffery's elementary school was involved with career awareness because his school district was participating in a joint initiative between the U.S. federal Departments of Labor and Education. Enacted into federal legislation in 1994, the School-to-Work Opportunities Act "provides venture capital to states and communities that compete to bring school-to-work programs into their neighborhoods." The administrators of Jeffery's district had competed successfully for this capital, adapting

New York State's Learning Standards for Career Development and Occupational Studies. (Pennsylvania standards for career and work were due September 2000, but were not yet available to districts.)

Jeffery and his K–12 peers face a curriculum aligned with the skill standards necessary to meet local industry and student needs. By high school, Jeffery will have a complete career map, carefully designed to ensure that he will acquire the necessary skills, knowledge, and deportment to succeed in the industry of his choice. Jeffery's mother and I talked for 30 minutes about writing and development. We traded stories about our fears for our children's education and future. She had already spoken with his teacher, who assured her that Jeffery was well within the norms of the class in writing and well ahead in other subjects. Jeffery had also successfully completed a course at a local private tutoring center where he had overcome an information processing problem in order to write more effectively. His mother, however, did not see progress on his latest essay. She told me that she was at her wits' end, and she had called to see if I (or someone else at the university) could help Jeffery (or her). My parting words were that the assignment seemed abstract for an 8-year-old to consider seriously.

Because I had promised to do so, I called Jeffery's teacher as a follow up. She explained that the curriculum was "a system of study that brought schools, industries, and communities together in order to bridge the gap between the current content of schooling and the skills needed in the workplace." Not missing a beat, she followed that statement with the notion that such programs were intended to increase the economic competitiveness of the United States. Working in an area hit hard by businesses moving their operations south and across national boundaries, Jeffery's teacher remarked that we must "do something for these kids." The district administrator with whom I spoke echoed this rationale and added that the extra funds available through the School-to-Work incentive program enabled the district to provide "basic knowledge, broad technical knowledge, and specialized job skills and knowledge" that would not be possible on their traditional state budget.

This seems a heavy burden for an 8-year-old to carry—to improve the competitiveness of the U.S. economy. Don't get me wrong, I know that children here and around the world carry burdens that are heavy indeed. When proofreading our daughter's presentation on child labor for a high school Amnesty International meeting, I learned that children Jeffery's age work in fields and factories in many parts of the world and that I am complicit in their laboring by the products I buy and the silence I keep.

Jeffery's teacher is not asking him to engage in physical labor. According to the skill-aligned curriculum, however, Jeffery is expected to direct a portion of his literacy toward acquiring the basic skills of industry. Not only is he to communicate in teams, prepare a poster, and follow written directions and protocols, but he must also become a pen pal with someone who works and inquire about his or her skills, read about people who work, and discuss what it takes to make an end product. Through these literacy practices, Jeffery is to develop an understanding of the changing nature of the workplace and to be able to describe which changes are based on globalism.

LITERACY AS COMMODITY

This skills-aligned curriculum transforms literacy from a human activity into a commodity that we can acquire and then later use to enhance our economic position. To be more precise, the entire school curriculum offers many uses of literacy. Jeffery is learning to read and write stories, history, mathematics, science, and music in different ways for differing purposes. Yet, the skills-aligned curriculum prioritizes those uses according to their putative values to industry. At the top of that list are the instrumental, regulatory, and heuristic uses that help students and workers get things done, control others, and find things out. Toward the bottom of that list are the personal, imaginative, and critical uses that help people express their personalities, create fantasy worlds, and understand themselves, others, and the society in which they live. I suppose that it is beneficial for Jeffery to exercise his utilitarian literacy, but I worry about the extra value placed on it in this program and the current rhetoric surrounding literacy education in U.S. schools.

Jeffery and his classmates are being asked to acquire literacy not for pleasure or citizenship. They are being asked to learn to read and write in particular ways because these ways are valued by business.

If students come to possess those valued uses of literacy, then they can sell them to employers who will then use the literacy (and the worker) as they see fit. According to this logic, valued literacy practices are transportable from job to job, rendering those who possess valued literacy powerful in the employment market. In this way, school-to-work curricula are a win–win situation. Jeffery and other American students improve their chances of employment and U.S. business's dominance in world markets through higher productivity.

In this logic, however, another transformation has taken place. Jeffery and his fellow students have also been changed to commodities. For it is not just the literacy that is being sold to employers, but Jeffery himself. As Berman (1998) put it, "The crucial reality is the need to sell your labor to capital in order to live, the need to carve up your personality for sale—to look at yourself in the mirror and think, 'What have I got that I can sell?' . . ." (p. 16). By definition, a commodity is a thing produced for sale. When we accept the school-to-work logic, curriculum, and funding, we engage in the transformation of literacy and students into commodities that can and will be sold to the highest bidder. When we assign Jeffery and others to write about what they want to be when they grow up, and we limit their options to the types of occupations they hope to fill, we mask these transformations in the apparent choice of what we will do with our lives.

SOMETHING NEEDS ATTENTION

As far as I can tell from my conversations with personnel in Jeffery's school district and from the scores of Web sites and government documents associated with school-to-work initiatives, little if any attention is paid to the use of literacy to analyze this masking and these transformations. Neither Jeffery nor his teacher are asked to slow down in order to consider what it means to prioritize literacy as a commodity, to treat schooling as preparation for work, and to project the problems we have created in the world upon our children.

I agreed to exchange e-mail messages with Jeffery in order to get a sense of his writing only if his mother would allow him to send them unedited. Here is his first e-mail: "Dear Mr. Shannon, My Dad says that you have hairy legs. Jeffery."

REFERENCE

Berman, M. 1998, May 11. "Unchained Melody." *The Nation*, pp. 11–17.

TEACHERS AS GRANTSEEKERS
The Privatization of the Urban Public School Teacher

SARA FREEDMAN

I was just a few minutes early for my interview with Maria Santos,[1] a bilingual special education teacher, but I could not figure out how to enter the school. We had arranged to meet in her classroom so that I could interview her in my role as the evaluator of a grant-funded professional development program that awards grants to teachers to develop curriculum materials and disseminate them to other teachers. I know how little time city teachers have during the school day outside of their teaching duties. I really didn't want to be late, but it didn't seem that I would ever be able to get inside. Most schools in this urban district are locked during the day. Many have several formal entrances that were used in years past but today are more ornamental than useful. The trick is to find one door with a small buzzer which, when pushed, summons someone from the office—often a small child—who is responsible for opening the door and screening all who wish to enter. Often no one ever comes.

Luckily, I saw a young woman approaching. As she opened one of the doors I slipped in behind her. She asked me whom I wanted to see and then gave me directions to Ms. Santos' room. I found out later that my guide was the principal. She asked me no questions, but seemed to regard visits to Maria as fairly commonplace. As I made my way, the corridors were quiet and orderly, dark with old, brown paint and lined with a mixture of 50 year old photographs and colorful art work from today's pupils.

I located Maria's small resource room up a flight of stairs and around to the side. Through the broken window panes that made up the upper part of her classroom door, I could see Maria sitting with her back to the hallway. I knocked. Without turning around, she signaled me to come in. She was busy typing on a portable mini-electronic typewriter. Next to her was a grant application. We had scheduled this meeting several weeks in advance, but Maria told me, somewhat apologetically, that she had only limited time to give me because she had a number of grant applications with deadlines this week.

This was the first time I saw how profound a change grantseeking had made in the life of teachers since I was laid off from my own job as a schoolteacher, fifteen years ago. Here was a teacher whose weekly, if not daily, routine was to write grants for herself and her school. There were enough grants to which she could apply that could keep her filling out such requests at the rate of two or three a week throughout the entire school year. The stark contrast between the very closed world of this teacher's school—literally locked away from the outside world—and the expansive, seemingly boundless world which corporate and private foundation sponsored grant competitions were apparently inviting urban teachers to enter—struck me with great force.

INTRODUCTION

As the above vignette suggests, grantseeking is a way of life in urban schools today. Specially designated development officers seek grants for district wide projects while enterprising principals and parents pursue grants for existing schools and programs and to provide startup funds for new "break the mold" enterprises. Teachers like Maria Santos, whose sanctioned role up to recent times has been confined almost exclusively to classroom activities and concerns, are also urged to take on the role of grantseekers to fund projects and materials for their individual classrooms and schools (Berns 1991; Bauer 1993; Richardson 1993; Novelli 1994) and to create and sustain networks to reform classroom practice and school structures (Useem 1995; Lieberman 1996).

The popular media and funding agencies, as well as many teachers, now promote the idea that the "good" teacher, especially the "good" urban teacher, accepts responsibility for and is adept at raising such funds for her classroom, her school, her school system, and her own professional development. Indeed, many of the other new roles created for teachers in the modern day reform movement—teacher as researcher/published author, teacher as mentor to colleagues and prospective teachers, teacher as curriculum developer, teacher as budget manager, personnel director, and project director depend upon teachers' abilities to "work the funding system" by meeting with foundation officers, writing award winning grants, establishing nationally recognized networks with other successful teacher/grantseekers and cooperating with public relations departments in publicizing grant-funded activities. Without the additional funds and perquisites grants provide to teachers, many of the new out-of-the-classroom roles now available to particular groups of teachers would simply not be possible (Little 1993; Hill 1993a; Etlin 1993; Useem 1995; Lieberman 1996).

Given the enormous increase in such programs and their potential impact upon individual teachers, their students, and their school systems, it is curious that little research attention has been directed at the role of private funding in supporting many of them, despite the fact that funding shifts from public to private in other areas of the educational system have been well documented and debated in the popular press and in the research community. The effort to place management of public schools in the hands of private corporations, for example, the move to create charter schools removed from public control and scrutiny and the provision of state funds for vouchers to be used in private schools have generated much debate (Chubb & Moe 1990; Wells et al. 1991; Lowe & Miner 1993; Cookson 1994; Fine 1994; Hakim et al. 1994; American Federation of Labor 1994; Saks 1995; Ascher et al. 1996; Richards et al. 1996; Hill et al. 1997; Freedman 1999). Less publicized has been the growth in private funding in education in the form of grant competitions that have increased inequities among individual schools and classrooms, particularly in urban school districts where many corporate and private foundations concentrate their K–12 funding efforts (Impact II 1989; Weisman 1992; Winerip 1993; Foundation Center 1996).

The Role of Grantseeking in the Movement to Privatize Public Education

I have conducted several studies in the past five years designed to explore the impact of private grantgiving on urban teachers. I first examined the most common type of grant program available to urban teachers in Northbridge,[2] a major city located in the eastern United States (Freedman 1989). I later expanded the study to include urban teachers' participation as grantseekers in several region wide, competitively selected grant programs designed to created networks of teacher leaders in the region in which Northbridge is located (Freedman 1993; Freedman 1994; Freedman

1996). I have reviewed over 500 grant applications submitted by individual teachers over the course of 15 years and examined extensive survey data collected from 125 teachers who participated in the region-wide network of teachers, ten of whom work in Northbridge. I have also conducted multiple return interviews with thirty teachers who work in the city's public school system and are among the most active teacher/grantseekers in the district.

On the basis of these studies, I argue that the growing participation of select groups of urban teachers in private grantgiving programs available to them on district, state and national levels has critical ideological, structural and cultural links to the movement to privatize public education (Gormley 1991; Hill 1997; Murphy 1996). I analyze the ways in which grantseeking promotes some of the central tenets of that movement among urban public school teachers—to "market" one's teaching as a product and oneself as a valuable commodity; to embrace competition and the creation of self-selected communities; and to replace a commitment to a broad-based democracy in which the needs of all are met with fulfilling the needs of the "deserving" few.

POTENTIAL BENEFITS AND DRAWBACKS OF GRANT FUNDED PROGRAMS TO URBAN TEACHERS

Benefits

In the Northbridge school system, a small minority of dedicated grantseekers within the general population of public school teachers has been remarkably successful in receiving grant funded awards on an almost continuous basis. In an urban district where many classrooms lack basic supplies, the classrooms of successful teacher/grantseekers are stocked with thousands, sometimes tens of thousands of dollars in computer equipment, telephone and satellite hook-ups, and in-class libraries of trade books, reference materials and CD-ROMs (Kantrowitz 1993; Hill 1993a; Hill 1993b). In addition to the obvious monetary advantages, such grants carry other distinct benefits for urban teachers. They promise teachers a measure of relief from the restrictions and bureaucratic roadblocks common to urban schools and the often degrading, unhealthy and appallingly hazardous conditions that many urban teachers and students endure on a daily basis. A veteran grantseeker comments on the leverage her success in fundraising has given her:

> When you go back to the schools you can say to the principal, which you couldn't say before, "No, I won't do that project you want me to do only because of the publicity you want. If you want me to do it, this is the way I want it. Otherwise I won't do it."

They provide a system-wide mechanism for publicly recognizing and rewarding those teachers who have successfully competed with their peers with little of the controversy and none of the contractual problems that proposals such as affirmative action, merit pay and differentiated staffing have elicited. As in other urban districts, competitive grant programs create networks for such Northbridge teachers beyond what is available to them within their individual schools, helping to break down the isolation endemic to teachers' working lives (Lieberman 1996; Pennell & Firestone 1996).

Drawbacks

Successful grantseeking, however, is not without drawbacks for those who participate as well as for those who do not. They do not promise a stable source of funding for the programs these teachers have developed, no matter how meritorious the programs on which they have worked. At the same time that teachers are increasingly urged to fund special programs for their individual classrooms, clusters and schools, there has been a reduction or total curtailment of discretionary funds provided by the public school system to teachers for materials and resources that are crucial to such "add ons" (Ribadeneira 1991; Hart 1992; Bean & Loar 1994). Individual teachers may not have the budget to buy even the basal reader mandated by the central administration despite the fact that students are tested and teachers evaluated on the progress students are making in mastering these texts (Schmidt 1991; Johnston 1997). One of the most successful teacher/grantseekers declares:

> I write them because I still want to be a good teacher and I want my kids to get a number one education and that's the only way that they're going to get it because the system . . . the city is not

going to give me the resources I need, so the only way I'm going to get these types of things in my classroom is to write grants to get them.

The underlying message is that the only way to gain the funds needed to teach effectively is to emulate the latest preferred program and hope to have one's classroom, cluster or school chosen as a model site, if only for a few years until another program catches the attention of individual funders or central administration or to create a school of one's own which will make the teacher again eligible for such funds (Winerip 1993; Leonard 1992; Instructor 1997).

In addition, the sheer proliferation of grants coming into a school as well as their conflicting purposes, sponsors and overlapping timetables often work to undermine and destablize the work of teachers—both those active in pursuing grants and those who are not—no matter how highly the teachers evaluate the merits of individual programs. Grant funded programs are sensitive to cycles of corporate boom and bust, proliferating when companies and the general economy appear strong and declining during recessions. Even when funds from specific private donors are assured, the grant program itself does not insure that teachers who were awarded grants can carry out the programs for which they received funds, or that they can do so under conditions similar to those existing when the grants were conceived and written. In periods of recurring layoffs and staff displacements interspersed with spurts of intensive hiring to which urban school systems have been particularly susceptible, grants have little or no effect on whether the teachers receiving them will retain their jobs or specific teaching positions.

A principal from the district told of a teacher who received notice of a grant award for a whole school project which she had conceived and spearheaded at the same time that she was reassigned to a different school. Another teacher comments on the bitter lesson she and other teachers in her school learned from that experience, feeling that the administration had encouraged the reassigned teacher to develop the project and write the grant without letting her know that she would probably not retain her position in the school:

> When people want to use you they want to use all the labor that you have produced and whatever but when it comes time

to any kind of credits or whatever they either take it or when there are problems, they turn around and blame you or don't support you. I just have been involved in so many things where people's jobs depended on things that I began to read other people's hidden agendas.

Thus, active grantseekers run the real risk of investing a great deal of time and emotional commitment to projects they may never be able to carry out or continue beyond the time frame of the initial grant (Cohen 1990).

Nor do grants always work to relieve the day to day isolation of the classroom teacher from other teachers, a condition long considered endemic to teaching and lamented by researchers, policy analysts, and teachers alike. Some teachers reported that while grantseeking has allowed them to develop strong bonds and alternative communities with other teachers outside of their buildings, it has also worked to distance them from the teachers in their own buildings and grade levels. One schism that has developed is that between those who feel comfortable writing in the particular formal style of grant proposals and have the time to do so, and those who do not. Successful grantseekers, while proud of their ability to pound out a winning grant under the very short turn around time that characterizes many of these grants, are also uneasy with the notion that a good grantwriter is necessarily a good teacher or, more importantly, that a good teacher is necessarily a good grantwriter.

> People are uncomfortable writing. That doesn't mean they are bad teachers. There is a person in this building who is a terrific teacher but she would never apply for a grant, even though she teaches writing and does a great job of it. Why does this person make all of these expectations for the kids when she won't do it herself?

Another successful grantseeker discusses this seeming paradox, acknowledging how difficult her own initial entry was into grantseeking and why writing to promote one's classroom and oneself is not a natural act for many urban teachers, the great majority of whom come from working class and lower middle class backgrounds like her own. She describes the way in which grantseeking assumes a specific kind of cultural capital that has historically been the hallmark and the road to advancement within middle class and upper middle class, male dominated professional positions—the ability to run meetings and conferences, to prepare publicity packages, to garner publicity for the teacher's program, to market that program, to write effective proposals and to meet with foundation directors as peers (Bourdieu 1977). The world of grantseeking has introduced this kind of cultural capital into teaching, establishing its various permutations as the accepted criteria for identifying exemplary teachers and rewarding them as most deserving. Until the advent of such grantgiving and grantseeking, this kind of cultural capital was not part of the world of many urban teachers, who more usually concentrate on day to day, emotionally and intellectually engulfing work with children. She explains:

> I went out of elementary school to high school to the state teachers college to a classroom and that's where I've stayed and that's where I've poured all my energy—with little kids, day after day. I never went in between that business world or that foundation world that people meet in and that some of the new teachers come from and then usually go back to pretty quickly. So when you're appalled that teachers like me can't write, when you're appalled that we can't speak or run meetings with bigwigs, it's because we've never done it before. And they really only choose a few of us to get the encouragement and the time to do it well enough to feel comfortable. And the worst thing would be to put out that effort, publicly, by going to all these introductory meetings, and then not get the grant.

In particular, teachers discussed the way in which relationships forged between white and African American teachers, relationships that have been tenuous at best in a district characterized by repeated layoffs and dislocations decided on racial lines, are endangered by such competitions and the underlying but never stated assumptions about who is and who isn't a good teacher according to the criteria established by such competitions. This is especially the case when grant programs limit the number of teachers from each building that can receive a grant award during each cycle.

Role of Teachers from Historically Oppressed Groups

Examining the role of teachers of color within grantseeking raises important issues to consider. Grantseeking, I would argue, is

dependent on the participation of teachers from historically oppressed groups within the United States such as Maria Santos,
albeit a small percentage within the larger group of successful
teacher/grantseekers, in order to gain legitimacy within the wider
teaching and educational community and to define it as a means
of addressing long-standing inequities and community concerns.
Teachers from historically oppressed groups who are best positioned
to receive such grants, who appear most amenable to the goals
and aspirations of the foundations awarding such grants and other
forms of privatizing public education, are by the nature of their
complex social positions exceptions to the general rule and "border crossers" (Anzaldua 1987). Border crossers bridge the gaps between the very different and often antagonistic worlds of privilege
and oppression found within and outside of schools in very public
and personally assertive ways. As Collins (1991) argues in the case
of Black women academics, rewards allocated by such border
crossers are designed to maintain rather than contest the status quo.

> One way of excluding the majority of Black women from the
> knowledge-validation process is to permit a few Black women
> to acquire positions of authority in institutions that legitimate
> knowledge and to encourage them to work within the taken-
> for-granted assumptions of Black female inferiority shared by
> the scholarly community and the culture at large. Those Black
> women who accept these assumptions are likely to be rewarded
> by their institutions, often at significant personal cost. Those
> challenging the assumptions run the risk of being ostracized
> (Collins 1991).

Grantseeking, I contend, has introduced the costs and tensions
Collins describes as experienced by border crossers within acade-
mia to the world of public elementary and secondary schools.
Grantseeking can be lonely, it can be schizophrenic, as well as
empowering and creative for a teacher such as Maria Santos. Possibly because she *is* a border crosser, at times she was able to tran-
scend the limitations of grantseeking in ways not envisioned nor
intended by those awarding the grants. At other times she was not.
Moreover, grant funded competitions continually attract and reward teachers from high status groups while marginalizing the contribution of teachers like Maria Santos when they choose to
emphasize their identification and commitment to historically op-

pressed communities. The majority of teachers working in inner city schools are peripheral to or very much removed from grantseeking and the community of teachers it fosters.

Role of Foundations and Other Grant-Awarding Bodies in Developing Competitive Grant Programs

By the mid 1980s businesses or private foundations began to pay for the great majority of "supplemental" programs that started to mark a school or teacher's offerings as unique and sustain its better-than-average test scores and other results that prove its status as an "effective" school (Hill 1993a; Madler 1996; Robles & Eversley 1996). As one director of a small magnet school in New York City commented:

> Magnets get tons of private contributions. . . . We are a niche within this vast sea of public education. A lot of businesses do not want to give to the traditional big-city school. They see it as throwing money down a well. (Winerip 1993).

This new wave of private fundings, led in no small part by the business interests that underwrote the national reports. Business interests recognized that additional funds for such "effective" schools were needed. They responded by supporting tax schemes and funding allocations that keep corporate taxes low while giving maximum publicity to individual corporate projects in a limited number of urban schools (Goertz 1990; Massachusetts Business Alliance for Education 1990; Molnar 1997).

> Many American companies in recent years have made a crusade of trying to rescue the nation's deteriorating public schools, casting themselves as white knights whose donations help the cause. But at the same time, many of these companies are extracting as many sizable tax breaks as they can from their communities, cutting off money needed to finance public education. (Celis 1991)

Funding to the public schools (Council for Aid to Education 1993) increased dramatically to support these new initiatives. Between 1984 and 1988 the number of business/education initiatives rose 234%—from 42,200 to 140,800 (Branch 1991). By the 1990s, prominent national corporations such as the Annenberg Foundation and the Lila Wallace/Readers' Digest Foundation began awarding unprecedented large sums of money to fund comprehensive plans in a number of cities across the country, combining large scale system wide reform efforts with individual school and teacher awards (Foundation Center 1996).

Through the grant award programs provided by such foundations and other school/business partnerships, businesses—at least to their own satisfaction—have proven their commitment to education and nurture a group within their own ranks with proprietary and vested interests in continuing and increasing business influence in the schools. At the same time, grant-funded projects, taken as a whole, have developed a track record as major players in education beyond the "narrow vocationalism" of the past when companies supported projects that directly served their own purposes (Business and the Public Schools Committee for Economic Development 1985; Weisman 1992, Molnar 1997).

As such funding patterns have accelerated, they have moved from the outer limits of the educational world to the center of educational debate and program development. Competitive grant award programs have thus become a major means of identifying, publicizing and developing new programs in schools, following the guidelines established by the awarding foundations or agencies. The grantseeking process now provides a mechanism by which foundations, for a limited amount of money, can decide exactly how many schools, school systems, and/or teachers they will fund, at what level of funding, and toward which goals. Using the modus operandi of venture capitalists operating in the private sector, these foundations retain the ability to shift funds quickly from one project to another, "hotter" project or teacher as interest in the now established program wanes—"just in time production" on a classroom-by-classroom, teacher-by-teacher, level.

Having acknowledged the resistance that organized teachers' groups have sustained against merit pay, differentiated staffing and affirmative action in Northbridge—all defined as stifling the autonomy and creativity of gifted teachers—the business community has greatly amplified the availability of competitive grants to individual teachers (Lobman 1992; Leonard 1992; Foundation Center 1996), thereby creating such hierarchies unofficially and without resistance. Grantseeking has thus become a well organized and accepted way for specific groups of urban teachers to translate the entrepreneurial model and cultural milieu of middle class professionalism into their own teaching situations.

The Enterprise of Grantseeking: Packaging and Marketing the "Product"

The fiscal structure of private foundations [and the tax laws that established them], as Leonard (1992) points out, create a strong incentive for private and corporate foundations to seek new projects and abandon old ones, no matter how meritorious they have proven to be. She writes,

> Foundations generally have a stable endowment and, therefore, a stable income, so that in order to fund new programs, they must discontinue old programs. This fact helps explain why most grants are restricted to two to five years, and why projects rather than institutions are the major beneficiaries of foundation help.

In order to comply with such financial and legal requirements, foundations structure grant funded competitions as a means of discovering ever new programs and product lines, much like corporations seeking new or enhanced product lines as a means of capturing new markets or retaining an existing client base. The majority of these grant competitions therefore ask teachers to compete not as classroom teachers but as curriculum developers. Given the limited time teachers have to develop these projects and the competing demands on their time, much of the material submitted as part of a teacher's curriculum project are those developed by a variety of sources, gathered and shaped by the teacher/demonstrator. Teachers are, however, required to describe these units as ones for which they can claim sole ownership, valorizing origination over adaptation and collaboration and having the simple good sense of being able to recognize good material and teach it effectively. In order to compete successfully in these contests and be identified as a successful teacher, they must adopt the strategies and writing style of the successful marketer and entrepreneur and to cast other teachers in the role of prospective consumers searching for "ready made" goods.

Nor are teachers always free to use the money as they might wish to use it, despite the oft-repeated rhetoric that private funds allow teachers and schools to develop programs to meet the needs that have been identified within the school by school staffs. Rather, teachers often feel the pressure to satisfy the "agendas," as they call them, of powerful private funding sources whose priorities as leaders in the field of school reform may compel them to establish goals quite different from those that would be set by the individual school or classroom teacher. One veteran teacher remarks:

> A lot of these grants have their own agendas and their own guidelines of what they want to have. Right now this fund wants their new grants to have a curricular component where they basically, not sell it, but it can be replicated. And I'm not sure that we need money in our school for that kind of thing. It's complicated. Yes, we want money for science, but no, we don't really want the money to write curriculum for other programs but to develop our programs here and convince teachers here to use them.

An entire industry has sprung up to meet the needs of school staff who wish to or are forced to participate in grantseeking. Grantseekers' guides for teachers and newly hired school development directors are now available. In the state in which Northbridge is located, the state's professional development office conducts a two-day grantsmanship institute specifically geared to teachers and individual school staffs. The institute provides workshops on how to search for grants, how to write successful grants, how to establish tax-exempt entities, and how to approach interested funders. Conspicuously missing is any critique of such funding patterns or the connections between the private foundations who fund these grants and their histories of fighting progressive tax programs.

CONCLUSION

The funding sources that award the grants, the general public, and to some extent teachers themselves have come to accept Maria Santos and other successful teacher/grantseekers as models of the "good" professional teacher. Such teachers combine the entrepreneurial spirit of competitive individualism with an old-fashioned devotion to meeting the needs of the pupils under their charge—the new professional woman combined, and in harmony, with the selfless, caring public servant and mother substitute.

Teacher/grantseekers have been featured in newspaper articles, interviewed and analyzed for research projects and evaluation studies (Kantrowitz 1993). Through the sponsorship of the grant programs and other competitions fostering other new reform initiated roles for teachers, many have established networks of other successful teacher/grantseekers they have met in national and regional conventions sponsored by the funders of these privately funded programs. They have come to demand their voices be heard in shaping and leading workshops and programs directed at teachers, with the expectation that they will play a central role in teacher development and school improvement projects (Impact II 1994). At the same time their position within their individual schools or districts is by no means stable, let alone assured.

None of these new roles as yet has officially and substantially removed the grantseekers from the classroom, but the trend is there, at least for a limited number of them. Dedicated teacher-grantseekers in this city school system spend more and more of their time both in and out of school doing what successful grantseekers do—researching what grants are available; consulting with various groups of people with whom they can collaborate on grants or from whom they can gain advice, expertise, encouragement and information crucial to their success as grantseekers; writing the grant applications; organizing and participating in programs funded by grants; and preparing final reports.

Most of the dedicated teacher-grantseekers now leave their classrooms at least two days a month as part of their involvement in grant funded programs. A number of them leave more frequently or for long periods of time. Maria Santos, for example, has been on a grant-funded sabbatical two out of the past four years. Active grantseekers recognize that if they remove themselves from the "loop" of grantseeking they will be left with few alternatives for providing the sustenance they now see as essential to their identity as successful teachers and a means of participating in the camaraderie and resource sharing such programs provide. "You are only as good as your last grant," commented one teacher.

Thus grantseeking sanctifies and celebrates a hierarchy within teaching which neatly mirrors the power structure within society at large, all under the guise of insuring more effective teaching to students of color. In the name of educational equity, a competitive process which limits access to vital funds that would support educational equity has been put into place. Grantseeking also works to reinforce a belief in meritocracy and the importance of rewarding the "best and the brightest." Ironically, such grant funded competitions mystify the notion of what it takes to write a successful grant application while at the same time often granting them to virtually everyone who applies—a fact unknown by many teachers not active as grantseekers. At the same time these programs steadfastly refuse to provide any concrete criteria for evaluating proposals other than if teachers filled out the necessary forms and directed their program to meet the focus of the particular grant competition. For example, neither the guidelines, the evaluators' instructions nor the evaluators' comments for the two grant programs whose statistics were discussed in this article—a local and a state program awarding grants to "exemplary" teachers—presented any coherent or consistent criteria used to select the applicants to whom the grants were awarded.

The applications did require prospective teacher demonstrators to list all grants they had received, past dissemination efforts, and their professional development activities. Teachers with an established track record in such programs received more points on their grant applications than those who had not previously received a grant—a veterans' preference if you will. In the few grant cycles in which a number of teachers who applied were denied grants, these extra points made the difference between those who received grants and those who did not.

What would grant-funded programs for teachers and schools—especially those targeting urban teachers—look like that would resolve the contradictions they have created? Or does the intrinsic nature of grantseeking prevent such resolutions and lead inevitably to some form of privatization? Given the fact that there is no organized movement inside or outside of schools that questions the very nature of grantfunding and the obstacles it creates to real and lasting improvement of urban public school education, these questions are difficult to answer.

The grant system celebrates meritocracy and the role of the individual teacher or school while evoking the promise of better, more equitable and more progressive schooling within the context of an ever more privatized system. It holds out to teachers the promise that if the funders of these competitions deem them worthy, they too can do what successful dedicated teacher/grantseekers do. At the same time, the widespread practice of grantseeking inherently withholds the means by which to develop and sustain a decent learning environment for their students from all but the most aggressive, most "deserving," few. Thus, the dynamics and intent of the grantseeking and grant awarding system forces individual teachers and staffs to compete against their next door neighbors or the next school for the limited number of grants awarded in such competitions. Grantseeking naturalizes the inequities such competitions create, even celebrates them as being in the best interests of all students. Through the magic of the marketplace, other teachers are expected now to seek similar rewards by entering similar contests, and as the theory goes, raise the level of education provided to all students.

Those urban teachers who are uncomfortable with such self-promotion, whose interests lie outside those established by such foundations, who feel intimidated by the formal writing requirements of the grant process or who simply do not have the time to attend the numerous information sessions, award ceremonies and corporate public relations events required by many of these programs are increasingly categorized as ineffective advocates for their own students no matter how effective they may be within their own classrooms, schools or communities. Thus, many grantseekers are acutely aware that the competitive system of grantseeking is designed precisely to institutionalize such inequities and reinforce such notions of meritocracy rather than redress them.

These trends are particularly ironic since many grant programs targeting urban school systems were developed initially to encourage teacher-to-teacher support and collaboration as an antidote to a perceived climate of stagnation and resignation and a much lamented lack of professionalism among rank and file teachers (Lortie 1975; Mann 1983; Cruickshank 1987). Thus, urban school systems are urged to implement programs that valorize the autonomy and professionalization of the individual teacher at the same time that they introduce programs to develop a community/school-based management approach. While the potential for conflict appears self-evident, and many teachers are acutely aware of

and deeply troubled by these two conflicting goals, school personnel are frequently reluctant to question publicly any program that
brings money into the schools and into their own classrooms. In
a system starved for funds, any source of funding is considered better than none—and any public discussion is widely viewed as tan-
tamount to treason and a clear sign of "unprofessional" behavior.

More troubling, the rising dominance of competitive grant programs in funding new programs or innovative programs has worked
to diminish the capacity of groups to contest or explore the nature
of the issues facing urban schools, while at the same time such
grant programs are trumpeted as enabling schools to do just that.
By requiring schools and individual teachers to write grant proposals in a way that emphasizes their ability to solve problems defined and targeted by the granting agency, foundations insure that
the "hidden curriculum" of grantfunding is never open to public
scrutiny or debate. To include any qualifications teachers might
have about the way the funder has defined the problem or established criteria for allocating its funds or to argue with the premises
of grant competitions themselves would be to effectively remove
one's program from any such competitions and the vital funds
they provide. Equally disturbing, grantseeking encourages teachers to narrow their interests and concerns to those that focus
solely on their individual classroom or school. Responding to
Requests for Proposals effectively suppresses any opportunity to
analyze the connections among the allocation of resources across
schools and communities, institutional racism and classism in the
larger society, and other public policy issues and community wide
concerns central to the life chances of their students and the communities in which those students live.

Many teachers in the urban school system in which this study
was conducted see the complexities and contradictions inherent
in grantseeking, along with other forms of privatization, but are
reluctant as individuals to jeopardize one of the few strategies that
has gained them a degree of autonomy, allowed them to develop
their own creativity and that of their students, and provided alternatives that could be the basis for system wide reforms. As long
as grant-funded programs are seen as models that ironically cannot
be duplicated but must be abandoned for ever newer ones—a model
that neatly emulates the marketplace ethos of grantseeking—the

progressive potential for many important and sorely needed reforms in urban education will never be realized. The real dangers grantseeking, as part of the movement toward the privatization of public education, presents to the reform of urban education will surely intensify and overwhelm any such reforms.

NOTES

1. Maria Santos is a pseudonym used to protect the confidentiality of the teacher whose experience is highlighted here.
2. Northbridge is a pseudonym for the city in which the studies on grantseeking were conducted.

REFERENCES

American Federation of Labor. 1994. *The Private Management of Public Schools: An Analysis of the EAI Experience in Baltimore*. Washington, DC: American Federation of Labor.

Anzaldua, G. 1987. *Borderlands/La frontera: The New Mestiza*. San Francisco: Spinters/Aunt Lute.

Ascher, C., Frucher, N., et al. 1996. *Hard Lessons: Public Schools and Privatization*. New York: Twentieth Century Fund.

Bauer, D. 1993. *Grantseeking Primer for Classroom Leaders*. New York: Scholastic.

Bean, J. & Loar, R. 1994, Dec. 16. "Funds Raised for Schools to Buy Extras May Be Used for Basics." *Los Angeles Times*. Sec A, p. 27.

Berns, B., Libby, B., & O'Connor, K. 1991. *A Teacher's Guide to Fellowships and Awards*. Washington, DC: Department of Education.

Bourdieu, P. 1977. *Outline of a Theory of Practice*. New York: Cambridge University Press.

Branch, E. 1991. "Can Business Save Schools?" *Black Enterprise*, 13 (3): 39–43.

Business and the Public Schools Committee for Economic Development. 1985. *Investing in Our Schools*. New York: New York Research and Policy Committee.

Celis, W. 1991, May 22. "Educators Press for End to Corporate Tax Breaks." *New York Times*, A1, B6.

Chubb, J., & Moe, T. 1990. *Politics, Markets, and America's Schools*. Washington, DC: Brookings Institute.

Cohen, M. 1990, May 8. "Layoff Notices Are Sent to 8,949 Teachers." *Globe*, 1, 10.

Collins, P. 1991. *Black Feminist Thought: Knowledge, Consciousness, and the Politics of Empowerment*. New York, Routledge.

Cookson, P. 1994. *School Choice: The Struggle for the Soul of American Education*. New Haven: Yale University Press.

Council for Aid to Education. 1993. *Corporate Support of Education, 1992*. New York: Council for Aid to Education.

Cruickshank, D. 1987. *Reflective Teaching*. Reston, VA: Association of Teacher Educators.

Etlin, M. 1993, April. "Private Foundations Lend Kids a Helping Hand." *NEA Today*, V.11, 8, p. 6.

Fine, M. ed. 1994. *Chartering Urban Schools: Reflections on Public High Schools in the Midst of Change*. New York: Teachers College Press.

Foundation Center. 1996. *Foundation Grant Index*. New York: Foundation Center.

Freedman, S. 1989. *Evaluation Report on Impact II*. Globe Foundation.

———. 1993. *Evaluation Report on the Academy for Teachers*. Institute for Teaching and Learning.

———. 1994. *Teachers as Grantseekers: Urban Women Teachers' Perceptions of Competitive Grant Programs for Individual Teachers*, unpublished dissertation, University of Massachusetts at Amherst.

———. 1996. "The Lure of Privatization: Public School Teachers Seeking Private Funds." *Discourse* (17) (December): 225–42.

———. 1999. "To Market, To Market: Privatizing Public Education." *Educational Policy*, 13 (3): 440–54.

Goertz, M. 1990. "Education Politics for a New Century: Introduction and Review." In *Education Politics for a New Century: The Twentieth Anniversary Politics of Education Yearbook*, edited by D. Mitchell & M. Goertz. London: Falmer Press.

Gormley, W. 1991. *Privatization and Its Alternatives*. Madison: University of Wisconsin Press.

Hakim, S., Seidenstat, P., & Bowman, G. eds. 1994. *Privatizing Education and Educational Choice: Concepts, Plans and Experience*. Westport, CT: Praeger.

Hart, J. 1992, January 5. "In Massachusetts, Teachers Fantasize About the Basics." *Boston Globe*, A53, A56.

Hill, D. 1993a. "California Dreamer." *Teacher Magazine, November/December*: 28–33.

Hill, D. 1993b. "Overnight Sensation: Kay Toliver." *Teacher Magazine, March*: 21–23.

Hill, P., Pierce, L., & Guthrie, J. 1997. *Reinventing Public Education: How Contracting Can Transform America's Schools*. Chicago: University of Chicago Press.

Impact II 1989. Meet Impact II. *Impact II National Network.* New York: Impact II.

———. 1994. How teachers are changing schools. New York: Impact II.

Instructor. 1997. "Win Those Grants." *Instructor,* 106 (5): 65.

Johnston, R. 1997, July 9. "Booming U.S. Economy Translates into Mixed Dividend for Education." *Education Week,* 48.

Kantrowitz, J. 1993, April 4. "Students Travel South." *Globe,* A55.

Leonard, M. 1992. "The Response of the Private Sector: Foundations and Entrepreneurs." *Teachers College Record, 93:* 376–81.

Lieberman, A. 1996. "Creating Intentional Learning Communities." *Educational Leadership* 51–55.

Little, J. 1993. "Professional Development in a Climate of Educational Reform." *Educational Evaluation and Policy Analysis* 15 (2): 129–51.

Lobman, T. 1992. "Public Education and Grant-Making Styles: More Money, More Vision, More Demands." *Teachers College Press, 93:* 382–402.

Lortie, D. 1975. *Schoolteacher.* Chicago: University of Chicago Press.

Lowe, R., & Miner, B. eds. 1993. *False Choices: Why School Vouchers Threaten Our Children's Future.* Milwaukee, WI: Rethinking Schools.

Madler, M. 1996, Sept. 9. "Foundations Step in for Needy School Districts." *Chicago Tribune,* Sec 2MC, p. 1.

Mann, D. 1983. "The Impact of IMPACT II." *Teachers College Press, 84:* 837–40.

Massachusetts Business Alliance for Education. 1990. *Status Report: March, 1990.* Boston: MBAE.

Molnar, A. 1997. *Giving Kids the Business: The Commercialization of America's Schools.* Boulder, CO: Westview Press.

Murphy, P. 1996. *The Privatization of Schooling: Problems and Possibilities.* New York: Corwin Press.

Novelli, J. July–Aug. 1994. "You Can Get Grants." *Instructor,* 104 (1): 33.

Pennell, J., and Firestone, W. 1996. "Changing Classroom Practices Through Teacher Networks: Matching Program Features with Teacher Characteristics and Circumstances." *Teachers College Record* 98 (1): 46–76.

Ribadeneira, D. 1991, Sept. 26. "Schools Office Blamed for Delays." *Globe,* 33, 38.

Richards, C., Shore, R. & Sawicky, M. 1996. *Risky Business: Private Management of Public Schools.* Washington, DC: Economic Policy Institute.

Richardson, J. 1993, May 5. "A Little Cash Helps 'Impact II' Teachers Make Reform Reality." *Education Week,* 1, 18.

Robles, J. & Eversley, M. 1996, Oct. 26. "Schools Get Huge Boost." *Detroit News and Free Press*, Sec. A, p. 1.

Saks, J. 1995. "Scrutinizing Edison." *American School Board Journal*, 182 (2): 20, 24, 25.

Schmidt, P. 1991, November 6. "Panel Urges Emergency Aid for Troubled Districts." *Education Week*, 17.

Useem, E. & others. 1995. "Urban Teacher Curriculum Networks and Systemic Change." Paper presented at annual meeting of the American Educational Research Association (San Francisco, CA, April 18–22).

Wells, A. S., Cookson Jr., P. W., Chubb, J. E., Moe, T. M., & Howe II, H. 1991. "Politics, Markets, and America's Schools: A Symposium." *Teachers College Press* 93 (1): 137–73.

Weisman, J. 1992, January 15. "Foundations Network Seeks to Spur Systemic Reform." *Education Week*, 15.

Winerip, M. 1993, Sept. 8. "In the Inner City, a Hungry Scramble for a Few Choice Classroom Seats." *New York Times*, B13.

SCHOOLING IN
CAPITALIST AMERICA

SAMUEL BOWLES AND HERBERT GINTIS

Since its inception in the United States, the public school system has been seen as a method of disciplining children in the
interest of producing a properly subordinate adult population.
Sometimes conscious and explicit, and at other times a natural
emanation from the conditions of dominance and subordinacy
prevalent in the economic sphere, the theme of social control per-
vades educational thought and policy. The forms of school discipline, the position of the teacher, and the moral conception of the
child have all changed over the years, but the overriding objective
has remained.

The most striking testimonial to the hegemony of the social
control ideology is perhaps its clear primacy even among those
who opposed such obvious manifestations of the authoritarian
classroom as corporal punishment and teacher-centered discussion.
The most progressive of progressive educators have shared the
common commitment to maintaining ultimate top-down control
over the child's activities. Indeed, much of the educational experimentation of the past century can be viewed as attempting to
broaden the discretion and deepen the involvement of the child
while maintaining hierarchical control over the ultimate processes
and outcomes of the educational encounter. The goal has been to
enhance student motivation while withholding effective participation in the setting of priorities.

Hence, like the view of the child, the concept of discipline has
itself changed. Two aspects of this change are particularly important. First, the once highly personalized authority of the teacher
has become a part of the bureaucratic structure of the modern
school. Unlike the teachers in the chaotic early nineteenth-century
district schools, modern teachers exercise less personal power and
rely more heavily on regulations promulgated by higher authori-
ties. Although frequently prey to arbitrary intervention by parents
and other community members, the nineteenth-century teacher
was the boss of the classroom. The modern teacher is in a more

ambiguous position. The very rules and regulations which add a patina of social authority to his or her commands at the same time rigidly circumscribe the teacher's freedom of action. Second, the aim of discipline is no longer mere compliance: the aim is now "behavior modification." Prompt and obedient response to bureaucratically sanctioned authority is, of course, a must. But sheer coercion is out of keeping with both the modern educator's view of the child and the larger social needs for a self-controlled—not just controlled—citizenry and work force. Discipline is still the theme, but the variations more often center on the "internalization of behavioral norms," on equipping the child with a built-in supervisor than on mere obedience to external authority and material sanctions.

The repressive nature of the schooling process is nowhere more clearly revealed than in the system of grading, the most basic process of allocating rewards within the school. We will have gone some distance toward comprehending the school as it is—in going behind the educational rhetoric—if we can answer the question: Who gets what and why?

Teachers are likely to reward those who conform to and strengthen the social order of the school with higher grades and approval, and punish violators with lower grades and other forms of disapproval, independent of their respective academic and cognitive accomplishments. This fact allows us to investigate exactly what personality traits, attitudes, and behavioral attributes are facilitated by the educational encounter.

Outside of gross disobedience, one would suspect the student's exhibition of creativity and divergence of thought to be most inimical to the smooth functioning of the hierarchical classroom. For the essence of the modern educational encounter is, to use Paulo Freire's words, that teaching:

> becomes an act of depositing, in which the students are the depositories and the teacher is the depositor. Instead of communicating, the teacher issues communiqués and makes deposits which the students patiently receive, memorize, and repeat. This is the "banking" concept of education. . . . The teacher teaches and the students are taught. . . . The teacher chooses and enforces his choice and the students comply. . . . The teacher acts

and the students have the illusion of acting through the action
of the teacher.[1]

Others refer to this conception as the "jug and mug" approach to
teaching whereby the jug fills up the mugs.

Thus the hostility of the school system to student behavior
even approaching critical consciousness should be evident in the
daily lives of students. Students are rewarded for exhibiting discipline, subordinacy, intellectually as opposed to emotionally oriented behavior, and hard work independent from intrinsic task
motivation. Moreover, these traits are rewarded independently of
any effect of "proper demeanor" on scholastic achievement.

Conformity to the social order of the school involves submis-
sion to a set of authority relationships which are inimical to personal growth. Instead of promoting a healthy balance among the
capacity for creative autonomy, diligence, and susceptibility to
social regulation, the reward system of the school inhibits those
manifestations of personal capacity which threaten hierarchical
authority.

We have emphasized elements of the "hidden curriculum" faced
in varying degrees by all students. But schools do different things
to different children. Boys and girls, blacks and whites, rich and
poor are treated differently. Affluent suburban schools, working-
class schools, and ghetto schools all exhibit a distinctive pattern
of sanctions and rewards. Moreover, most of the discussion here
has focused on high-school students. In important ways, colleges
are different; and community colleges exhibit social relations of
education which differ sharply from those of elite four-year institutions. In short, U.S. education is not monolithic.

Why do schools reward docility, passivity, and obedience? Why
do they penalize creativity and spontaneity? Why the historical
constancy of suppression and domination in an institution so central to the elevation of youth? Surely this is a glaring anomaly in
terms of traditional liberal educational theory. The naive enthusiasm of the contemporary free-school movement suggests the
implicit assumption that no one had ever tried to correct this situation—that the ideal of liberated education is simply a new conception which has never been tried. Even sophisticated critics,

such as Charles Silberman, tend to attribute the oppressiveness of schooling to simple oversight and irrationality:

> What is mostly wrong with public schools is not due to venal-
> ity or indifference or stupidity but to mindlessness. . . . It simply
> never occurs to more than a handful, to ask why they are doing
> what they are doing—to think seriously or deeply about the
> purposes or consequences of education.[2]

Yet, the history of the progressive-education movement attests to the intransigence of the educational system to "enlightened change" within the context of corporate capitalism.

We believe the available evidence indicates that the pattern of social relationships fostered in schools is hardly irrational or acci- dental. Rather, the structure of the educational experience is ad- mirably suited to nurturing attitudes and behavior consonant with participation in the labor force. Particularly dramatic is the statis- tically verifiable congruence between the personality traits con- ducive to proper work performance on the job and those which are rewarded with high grades in the classroom.

Capitalist production, in our view, is not simply a technical process; it is also a social process. Workers are neither machines nor commodities but, rather, active human beings who participate in production with the aim of satisfying their personal and social needs. The central problem of the employer is to erect a set of so- cial relationships and organizational forms, both within the en- terprise and, if possible, in society at large, that will channel these aims into the production and expropriation of surplus value. Thus as a social process, capitalist production is inherently antagonistic and always potentially explosive. Though class conflicts take many forms, the most basic occurs in this struggle over the creation and expropriation of surplus value.

It is immediately evident that profits will be greater, the lower is the total wage bill paid by the employer and the greater is the productivity and intensity of labor. Education in the United States plays a dual role in the social process whereby surplus value, i.e., profit, is created and expropriated. On the one hand, by im- parting technical and social skills and appropriate motivations, education increases the productive capacity of workers. On the other hand, education helps defuse and depoliticize the potentially explosive class relations of the production process, and thus serves to perpetuate the social, political, and economic conditions through which a portion of the product of labor is expropriated in the form of profits.

This simple model, reflecting the undemocratic and class-based character of economic life in the United States, bears a number of central implications:

First, we find that prevailing degrees of economic inequality and types of personal development are defined primarily by the market, property, and power relationships which define the capitalist system. Moreover, basic changes in the degree of inequality and in socially directed forms of personal development occur almost exclusively—if sometimes indirectly—through the normal process of capital accumulation and economic growth, and through shifts in the power among groups engaged in economic activity.

Second, the educational system does not add to or subtract from the overall degree of inequality and repressive personal development. Rather, it is best understood as an institution which serves to perpetuate the social relationships of economic life through which these patterns are set, by facilitating a smooth integration of youth into the labor force. This role takes a variety of forms. Schools legitimate inequality through the ostensibly meritocratic manner by which they reward and promote students, and allocate them to distinct positions in the occupational hierarchy. They create and reinforce patterns of social class and racial and sexual identification among students which allow them to relate "properly" to their eventual standing in the hierarchy of authority and status in the production process. Schools foster types of personal development compatible with the relationships of dominance and subordinacy in the economic sphere, and finally, schools create surpluses of skilled labor sufficiently extensive to render effective the prime weapon of the employer in disciplining labor—the power to hire and fire.

Third, the educational system operates in this manner not so much through the conscious intentions of teachers and administrators in their day-to-day activities, but through a close correspondence between the social relationships which govern personal interaction in the workplace and the social relationships of the educational system. Specifically, the relationships of authority and control between administrators and teachers, teachers and students, students and students, and students and their workplace. Power is organized along vertical lines of authority from administration to faculty to student body; students have a degree of control over their curriculum comparable to that of the worker over the content of his job. The motivational system of the school, involving as it does grades and other external rewards and the threat of failure rather than the intrinsic social benefits of the process of education (learning) or its tangible outcome (knowledge), mirrors closely the role of wages and the specter of unemployment in the motivation of workers. The fragmented nature of jobs is reflected in the institutionalized and rarely constructive competition among students and in the specialization and compartmentalization of academic knowledge. Finally, the relationships of dominance and subordinacy in education differ by level. The rule orientation of the high school reflects the close supervision of low-level workers; the internalization of norms and freedom from continual supervision in elite colleges reflect the social relationships of upper-level white-collar work. Most state universities and community colleges, which fall in between, conform to the behavioral requisites of low-level technical, service, and supervisory personnel.

Fourth, though the school system has effectively served the interests of profit and political stability, it has hardly been a finely tuned instrument of manipulation in the hands of socially dominant groups. Schools and colleges do indeed help to justify inequality, but they also have become arenas in which a highly politicized egalitarian consciousness has developed among some parents, teachers, and students. The authoritarian classroom does produce docile workers, but it also produces misfits and rebels. The university trains the elite in the skills of domination, but it has also given birth to a powerful radical movement and critique of capitalist society. The contradictory nature of U.S. education stems in part from the fact that the imperatives of profit often pull the school system in opposite directions. The types of training required to develop productive workers are often ill suited to the perpetuation of those ideas and institutions which facilitate the profitable employment of labor. Furthermore, contradictory forces external to the school system continually impinge upon its operations. Students, working people, parents, and others have attempted to use education to attain a greater share of the social wealth, to develop genuinely critical capacities, to gain material security, in short to pursue objectives different from—and often diametrically opposed to—those of capital. Education in the United States is as contradictory and complex as the larger society; no simplistic or mechanical theory can help us understand it.

NOTES

1. Paulo Freire, *Pedagogy of the Oppressed* (New York: Herder and Herder, 1972), 58–59.
2. Charles Silberman, *Crisis in the Classroom* (New York: Vintage, 1971), 10, 11.

III

PRIVATIZATION OF SCHOOLS

Over the last few years, the center of gravity for American education has shifted from local schools and districts to state capitals. The commissioner or state superintendent of schools, the state board of education, and the legislature have usurped much of the power that communities have long enjoyed to set education policy. Indeed, even Washington, DC, has gotten into the act, with new federal legislation requiring that every state test every student every year.

It's understandable, then, that frustrated students, parents, and teachers would be inclined to see government as the problem. Some conservative activists have even begun referring derisively to public schools as "government schools." But there are two problems with this equation. First, the current level of interference in curricular and assessment decisions on the part of politicians is not logically entailed by the idea of public schooling; indeed, it is unprecedented. If your governor began telling your local library which books to order, that would not be an argument against the idea of public libraries. Second, the actions taken by government officials have been offensive precisely to the extent that they have appropriated the slogans and mind-set of private enterprise. The problem is that people in the public sector are uncritically adopting the worldview of the private sector—and applying it to schools.

Many public officials have even come to support efforts to privatize education altogether. This movement repudiates the core principle that "a democratic culture cannot survive unless schooling gets treated as a public good rather than a private good," in the words of this section's first contributor, Henry A. Giroux. The privatization movement seems to be gathering strength as people friendly to its aims find themselves in positions of power, as the

Supreme Court narrowly voted in June 2002 to allow public funds to pay for tuition at private—including religious—schools, and as proponents become more skilled at public relations (for example, jettisoning the unpopular word *vouchers* and justifying their agenda in terms of its ostensible benefits for low-income people of color).

Privatizing schools is predicated on an almost childlike faith in competition: Let self-interested people struggle against one another, and somehow all of them will benefit. This belief, as quickly becomes evident from reading and listening to those who hold it, has the status of religious dogma rather than empirical hypothesis. It is closely related to a second ideological underpinning: a pronounced individualism in which there is no us, just you and her and him and me. To apply a marketplace mentality to education both assumes and exacerbates this perspective, with parents encouraged to focus only on what improves their own children's position. This is the very opposite of an invitation to work together to make schools more effective and inviting places for all our children. In fact, it might be construed as a challenge to the very idea of democracy as a political and social ideal, which embraces the value of community.

Clearly, education is just one arena in which larger ideologies are being played out. These days, as education historian David Labaree put it, "We find public schools under attack, not just because they are deemed ineffective, but because they are public."[1] Once the struggle over public institutions has been joined in the classroom, though, it isn't hard to understand the consequences of implementing voucher plans and other "school choice" proposals—including, perhaps, charter schools, which some see as a first step toward undermining public schooling altogether.

What happens to schools when they are plunged into the marketplace? To begin with, they must shift much of their time and resources to, well, marketing. (It is those who sell themselves skillfully, not those who are especially good at what they do, who tend to succeed in a competitive market.) Moreover, the pressure to make themselves look better presents a temptation to screen out less desirable students, those whose education takes more effort or expense. "The problem with public schools," remarked author John Chubb, "is that they must take whoever walks in the door."[2] The philosophical core of the privatization movement for which

Chubb speaks is neatly contained in the use of the word *problem* in that sentence.

Deborah Meier speaks memorably of the "dictatorship of the marketplace," noting that "privatizing removes schools from democratic control." She observes that private schools "cannot serve as general models; their value and advantages depend on their scarcity. . . . Schools dependent upon private clienteles—schools that can get rid of unwanted kids or troublemaker families . . . and toss aside the losers—not only can avoid the democratic arts of compromise and tolerance but also implicitly foster lessons about the power of money and prestige, a lesson already too well-known by every adolescent in America."[3]

In its entirety, Meier's indictment extends beyond voucher programs, suggesting the corrosive effect of any sort of interference in public education by business interests. The quest for private profits, in whatever form it takes, can only contaminate efforts to help all students become enthusiastic and expert learners, she insists. Her words are worth quoting at greater length, as are those of many other writers. For example, I wish we had been able to reprint accounts of other countries' experiences with school choice programs. (The results are disconcerting, to say the least.[4]) But as it is, I think we have assembled a collection of cogent critiques. Giroux ties together many of the strands of this book, offering a ringing defense of public education at a time when it is under attack. Robert Lowe presents a brief history of voucher proposals, debunking some claims offered in their behalf. Barbara Miner reviews some of the latest developments in—and problems with—the attempts of for-profit companies to manage public schools. Makani Themba explores the racial resonance of school choice, reminding us that "this country's first school voucher movement gave public dollars to white students in Virginia to attend private, segregated schools." Finally, Kenneth Howe and his colleagues present a case study of one district's experience with a choice plan, concluding that it has not led to "an overall improvement in achievement" but rather created "a situation in which some schools do better only at the expense of others that do worse." That outcome alone is reason to oppose turning learning into a business.

—Alfie Kohn

NOTES

1. David F. Labaree, *How to Succeed in School Without Really Learning: The Credentials Race in American Education* (New Haven: Yale University Press, 1997), p. 51.

2. Chubb (more about whom on pp. 120–24) is quoted in Bernie Froese-Germain, "What We Know About School Choice," *Education Canada*, Fall 1998, p. 22.

3. Deborah Meier, *The Power of Their Ideas* (Boston: Beacon, 1995), pp. 79, 8, 104, 7.

4. For example, see Martin Carnoy's account of Chile in "Is School Privatization the Answer?" *Education Week*, July 12, 1995, pp. 52, 40; and Edward B. Fiske and Helen F. Ladd's account of New Zealand in *When Schools Compete: A Cautionary Tale* (Washington, DC: Brookings Institution Press, 2000), or their article "A Distant Laboratory," *Education Week*, May 17, 2000, pp. 56, 38.

SCHOOLS FOR SALE
Public Education, Corporate Culture, and the Citizen-Consumer

HENRY A. GIROUX

If one-quarter of the products made on an assembly line do not work and another quarter fall off the line, the solution is not to run the line faster or longer. Different production processes must be created. Is it so different for our education system? In the United States, and throughout the world, we need new ways to conduct the business of educating the young, and entrepreneurship must be at the top of any list of reforms (Doyle 1994).

A venerable political and philosophical tradition extends from Thomas Jefferson to C. Wright Mills extolling public education as essential to a vibrant democracy. Central to this tradition is the assumption that a democratic culture cannot survive unless schooling gets treated as a public good rather than a private good. Today, this legacy of public discourse appears to have faded. U.S. educational consultants, from Robert Zemsky of Stanford University to Chester Finn Jr. of the Hudson Institute, "advise their clients in the name of efficiency to act like corporations selling products and seek 'market niches' to save themselves" (Aronowitz 1998, 32). In this way, it is argued, schools can meet the challenges of the new-world economic order.

Defining schools primarily through an appeal to the fulfillment of individual needs and the market registers of commercial investment and profit, advocates of corporate culture no longer view public education in terms of its civic function. Instead, they view education primarily as a commercial venture in which the only form of citizenship offered to young people is consumerism. Yet reducing public education to the ideological imperatives of corporate culture works against the critical social demands of educating citizens who can sustain and develop inclusive democratic identities, relations, and public spheres. The struggle to reclaim public schools must be seen as part of a broader battle over the defense of the public good. At the heart of such a struggle is the need to challenge the ever-growing discourse and influence of corporate culture, power, and politics.

PRIVATIZING AND COMMERCIALIZING PUBLIC SCHOOLS

The corporatizing of public education has taken a distinct turn approaching the 21st century. No longer content to argue for the application of business principles to the organization of schooling, the forces of corporate culture have adopted a more radical agenda for public education. Central to this agenda is the attempt to transform public education from a public good, benefiting all students, to a private good designed to expand the profits of investors, educate students as consumers, and train young people for the low-paying jobs of the new global marketplace. Though advocates of marketplace-based approaches to schooling offer a range of diverse theoretical positions, they share a faith in corporate culture. The culture they present overwhelms any defense of public education as a non-commodified public sphere, a repository for nourishing the primacy of civic over corporate values, or a public entitlement essential for the well-being of children and the future of democracy.

Privatization is the most powerful educational reform movement. An array of conservative institutions—including the Heritage Foundation, Hudson Institute, and the Olin Foundation— funds the privatization movement (Vine 1997). Capitalizing on its wealth and media influence, these groups have enlisted an army of conservative pundits, many of whom served in the U.S. Department of Education under Presidents Reagan and Bush [senior]. Some of the better-known members of this reform movement include Chester Finn Jr., Lamar Alexander, Diane Ravitch, David Kearns, and William Bennett. Providing policy papers and op-ed commentaries, appearing on television talk shows, and running a variety of educational clearinghouses and resource centers, these stalwart opponents of public education relentlessly blame schools for the country's economic woes. Citing low test scores, a decline in basic skills, and the watering down of the school curriculum

Ravitch (1995) and Finn and Kirkpatrick (1990) have legit-
imized the ideology of privatization and its accompanying call for
vouchers, privatized charter schools, and the placing of public
schools in the control of corporate contractors. Many of these reports are produced by right-wing think tanks with a vested interest in the privatization movement (Perkin 1998; Berliner and
Biddle 1995; Bracey 1997). Most specific reforms simply recycle
right-wing critiques calling for the replacement of teacher unions
and "giving parents choice, back-to-basics and performance-driven curriculums, management 'design teams,' and accountability" (Vine 1997, 12).

Underlying the call for privatization is a reform movement that
views public education as "a local industry that over time will become a global business" (Vine 1997, 12). As a for-profit venture,
public education represents a market worth more than $600 bil-
lion. The importance of such a market has not been lost on conservatives such as Chester Finn Jr. and David Kearns, both of
whom have connections with for-profit schooling groups such as
the Edison Project and the North American Schools Development
Corporation. At the policy level, the right-wing assault has been
quite successful. More than 28 states have drafted legislation supporting vouchers, choice programs, and contracting with for-profit
management companies such as the Edison Project and Sabis International Schools. The public's perception of such ventures,
however, appears to be less enthusiastic—and rightly so. Many
firms, such as Education Alternatives, Inc., which took over public schools in Hartford and Baltimore, have had their contracts
canceled due to numerous public complaints. The complaints range
from the way firms handle kids with learning disabilities and engage in union busting to how their cookie-cutter standardized curriculum and testing packages fail to provide promised educational
results (Ascher, Fruchter, and Berne 1996; Shapiro 1996).

There is, of course, more at stake in the privatization of public
schooling than issues of public versus private ownership or public
good versus private gain. We must weigh individual achievement
against equity and the social good. We must decide how teaching
and learning get defined. We must ask what identities are produced in defining students' histories, experiences, values, and desires through corporate rather than democratic ideals.

Within the language of privatization and market reforms, a strong emphasis exists on standards, measurements of outcomes, and holding teachers and students more accountable. Privatization is an appealing prospect for legislators who do not want to spend taxpayers' money on schools and for those who do not want to support education through increased taxes. These appeals are reductive in nature and hollow in substance. They remove questions of equity and equality from the discourse of standards. Furthermore, they appropriate the democratic rhetoric of choice and freedom without addressing issues of power. By refusing to address financial inequities that burden public schools, the ideas and images permeating this corporate model of schooling reek with the rhetoric of insincerity and the politics of social indifference. Kozol (1997, 16) captured this sentiment well:

> To speak of national standards and, increasingly, of national exams but never to dare speak of national equality is a transparent venture into punitive hypocrisy. Thus, the children in poor rural schools in Mississippi and Ohio will continue to get education funded at less than $4,000 yearly and children in the South Bronx will get less than $7,000, while children in the richest suburbs will continue to receive up to $18,000 yearly. But they'll all be told they must be held to the same standards and they'll all be judged, of course, by their performance on the same exams.

Stripped of a language of social responsibility advocates of privatization reject the assumption that school failure might be better understood within the political, economic, and social dynamics of poverty, joblessness, sexism, race and class discrimination, unequal funding, or a diminished tax base. Student failure, especially the failure of poor minority-group students, is instead often attributed to a genetically encoded lack of intelligence, a culture of deprivation, or pathology. Books such as The Bell Curve (Herrnstein and Murray 1994), as well as films such as 187 and Dangerous Minds, reinforce negative representations about urban African-American and Latino youths. These works perpetuate a history of racist exclusions being deepened by the informalities of privatization schemes in which schools mimic the free market and competitive spirit allows the most motivated and gifted students to succeed. A shameful element of racism and a retrograde Social

Darwinism permeate this discourse, relinquishing the responsibility of parents, teachers, administrators, social workers, business people, and the wider society. These groups must provide all young people with the cultural resources, economic opportunities, and social services necessary to learn without having to bear the crushing burdens of poverty, racism, and other forms of oppression.

The excessive celebration of individual sovereignty does more than remove the dynamics of student performance from broader social and political considerations. It also feeds a value system in which a definition of education exclusively as a private good displaces compassion, solidarity, cooperation, social responsibility, and other attributes of education as a social good. If education includes, partly, the creation of particular identities, the corporate model privileges a notion of the student as an individual consumer. As Labaree (1997, 48) noted, education in a consumerist system

> is a private good that only benefits the owner, an investment in my future, not yours, in my children, not other people's children. For such an educational system to work effectively, it needs to focus a lot of attention on grading, sorting, and selecting students. It needs to provide a variety of ways for individuals to distinguish themselves from others—such as by placing themselves in a more prestigious college, a higher curriculum track, the top reading group, or the gifted program.

Education in this framework becomes less a social investment than an individual investment. It is a vehicle for social mobility for those privileged to have the sources and power to make their choices matter. This type of educational system also acts as a form of social constraint for those who lack resources and for whom choice and accountability betray the legacy of broken promise and an ideology of bad faith.

The privatization model of schooling defaults on the legacy schooling as a public good by undermining the power of teachers to provide students with the vocabulary and skills of responsible citizenship. Under the drive to impose national curricular uniformity and standardized testing, advocates of privatization devalue teacher authority. Indeed, these advocates *de*-skill teachers by dictating not only what to teach but how they should teach. California, for example, is drafting legislation that mandates both the content of school knowledge and "more specific guidelines for when and how to teach various principles in the core subjects" (Manzo 1998, 7). Teaching in this perspective is completely removed from the cultural and social contexts shaping particular traditions, histories, and experiences in a community and school. Hence, there can be no recognition in this model of educational reform that students come from different backgrounds, bring diverse cultural experiences, and relate to the world in different ways. There is no sense in this approach of what it means for teachers to make knowledge meaningful, critical, and transformative. Pedagogical importance is no longer placed on having teachers begin with "where people are and how they actually live their lives" (Grossberg 1997, 257). Rather, teaching in the corporate model redefines importance by emphasizing the translation of educational exchange into financial exchange. Acknowledging students' histories—the stories that inform their lives—and weaving such information into webs of meaning that link the everyday with the academic is a powerful way to make knowledge meaningful. Yet teachers who take this approach cannot be expected to standardize, routinize, or reduce learning to a prepackaged curriculum, because it takes seriously the abilities of teachers to theorize, contextualize, and honor the diverse lives of their students.

A debilitating logic is at work in the corporate model of teaching with its mandated curriculum, top-down teaching practices, and national tests to measure educational standards. Infused with the drive toward standardized curricula and teaching, schools defeat their own goals. As Meier (1997, 24) noted, "Teachers and communities shorn of the capacity to use their own ideas, judgments and initiative in matters of importance can't teach kids to do so." Such pedagogical approaches have little to do with teaching responsible citizenship; instead, they redefine teaching as less an intellectual activity and more a depoliticized, de-skilled clerkship. The main role of the teacher-turned-classroom manager is to legitimize through mandated subject matter and pedagogical practices a market-based conception of the learner as a mere consumer of information. These reforms have support despite a tradition of critique addressing the ways in which teachers are being de-skilled and treated "more and more as impersonal instruments in a bureaucratic process than as thoughtful and creative intellectuals whose personal vision of education really matters" (Shapiro 1998, 54). Moreover, the standardized teaching models proffered by corporations make it difficult to offer students the opportunity to think critically about the knowledge they gain. These students cannot appreciate the value of learning as more than mastering discrete bits of information or learn to use knowledge as a form of power. Significantly, privatization celebrates competitive, self-interested individuals attempting to further their own needs and aspirations. It also takes place within a discourse of cultural decline—a jeremiad against public life—and in doing so actually undermines the role that public schools might play in keeping the experiences, hopes, and dreams of a democracy alive for each successive generation of students.

While the discourse of privatization has as its major objective conformity of public schools to the needs of the market and reflects more completely the interests of corporate culture, its goals are not limited to relocating the wholesale ownership and control of public schools to the private sector. This goal represents the most direct assault on schooling as a public sphere. A different but no less important and dangerous strategy of the corporate dismantling and takeover of public schools is the promotion of educational choice, vouchers, and charters as ways to open public schools to private contractors and use taxes to finance the creation of private forms of education. The real danger of privatization, as Henig (1996, 11) noted, is not that students who transfer into private schools will drain money from the public schools; rather, the risk is that they will further a process already at work in the larger society aimed at eroding "the public forums in which decisions with social consequences can be democratically resolved."

The commercial logic that fuels this market-based reform movement is also evident in the way corporate culture targets schools both as investments for substantial profits and as training grounds for educating students to define themselves as consumers rather than as multifaceted social actors. The marriage of commercialism and pedagogy often takes place in schools with too few resources to monitor the structure of learning critically. As schools struggle to raise money for texts, curricula, and extracurricular activities, they engage in partnerships with businesses all too willing to provide free curricular packages. Channel One, for example, provides schools with $50,000 in "free" electronic equipment—including videocassette recorders, televisions, and satellite dishes—on the condition that they broadcast a ten-minute program of current events and news material along with two minutes of commercials.

In Broward County, Florida, Pembroke Lakes Elementary School has adopted a curriculum package sponsored by McDonald's Corporation. Wechsler (1997, 69) reported that ten-year-old "Travis Licate recently learned how to design a McDonald's restaurant, how a McDonald's works, and how to apply and interview for a job at McDonald's thanks to [the] seven-week company sponsored class intended to teach kids about the work world." When asked if the curriculum was worthwhile, Licate responded, "if you want to work in a McDonald's when you grow up, you already know what to do. . . . Also, McDonald's is better than Burger King" (Wechsler 1997, 69). According to the Center for Commercial-Free Public Education (1998), Exxon Chemical Company developed a curriculum that teaches students that the Exxon *Valdez* oil spill was an example of environmental protection. A curriculum sponsored by Nike Inc. teaches students to learn about the creation of a Nike shoe but fails to address "the sweatshop portion of the manufacturing process" (Center for Commercial-Free Public Education 1998, 16). Schools often lack critical resources for recognizing the sleight of hand masquerading as a generous offer on the part of corporations willing to provide curricular packages or rent space. Such curricula have little to do with critical learning and a great deal with shaping students' identities, dreams, and desires within the limited and debilitating image of preparing for work and life in the fast-food and service industries.

Caught in a financial crunch, many school systems go beyond mere acceptance of corporate-sponsored curricula. Some lease space in their hallways, on their buses, and even on book covers. Cover Concepts Marketing Services, Inc., for example, provides schools with free book covers strategically designed to promote brand-name products such as Nike, Gitano, Foot Locker, Starburst, Nestlé, and Pepsi. The covers are distributed to more than 8,000 public schools and reach an audience of more than 6 million high school, junior high, and elementary school students (Consumer Union of the United States 1995). In Colorado Springs, Palmer

High School allows advertisements for Burger King and Sprite on the sides of its school buses. In Salt Lake City, Youthtalk Advertising Agency places acrylic-faced advertising billboards in school restrooms and cafeterias. The company estimates that more than "80,000 students are exposed to the ads while standing at urinals and sitting in toilet stalls" (Consumer Union of the United States 1995, 26).

Schools have condoned a transformation to commercial spheres while undermining—if not discarding—their role as public spheres. Their students become subject to the whims and practices of marketers whose agenda has nothing to do with critical learning and a great deal to do with restructuring civic life in the image of market culture (Molnar 1996, Kincheloe and Steinberg 1997). Civic courage as a defining principle of civil society in this context is utterly devalued. Corporate power transforms school knowledge, teaching students to recognize brand names or learn the appropriate attitudes for future work in low-skilled, low-paying jobs. Students do not learn how to connect the meaning of work to the imperatives of a strong democracy. Channel One, Nike, Pepsi, the Campbell Soup Company, McDonald's, and a host of other corporations substitute corporate propaganda for real learning, upset the balance between the public and the private, and treat schools like any other business.

Underlying the attempt to redefine the meaning and purpose of schooling as part of a market economy rather than a fundamental feature of substantive democracy is a model of society in which "consumer accountability [is] mediated by a relationship with an educational market [rather than] a democratic accountability mediated by a relationship with the whole community of citizens" (Grace 1997, 314). Most disturbing about the market approach to schooling is that it contains no special consideration for the vocabulary of ethics and values. Grace (1997) has warned that, when public education becomes a venue for making a profit, delivering a product, or constructing commodity-hungry subjects, education reneges on its responsibilities for creating a democracy of citizens by shifting its focus on producing a democracy of consumers. The corporate model of schooling and the market culture it legitimizes undermine the traditional notion that schools are the most visible symbols for educating students in the skills of leadership, citizenship, and democracy. Indeed, the current educational reform movement must be recognized as a full-fledged attack on both public education and democracy itself. As Stratman (1998, 7) has cautioned, the goal of such a movement "is not to raise the expectations of our young people but to narrow, stifle, and crush them." Anyone concerned about public education and the fundamental role it should play in placing limits on market culture, affirming the language of moral compassion, and expanding the meaning of freedom and choice to broader considerations of equity, justice, and social responsibility should heed Stratman's message.

EDUCATION AND THE IMPERATIVES OF DEMOCRACY

Challenging the encroachment of corporate power becomes essential if democracy is to remain a defining principle of education and everyday life. Part of such a challenge necessitates that educators and others create organizations capable of mobilizing civic dialogue, providing an alternative conception of the meaning and purpose of public education, and organizing to produce legislation to challenge corporate power's ascendancy over the institutions and mechanisms of civil society. Educators, students, and members of the community will have to provide the rationale and mobilize to create enclaves of resistance, new public cultures for collective development, and institutional spaces that highlight, nourish, and evaluate the tension between civil society and corporate power. They must also prioritize citizen rights over consumer rights.

Strategically, revitalizing public dialogue suggests that educators must take seriously the importance of defending public education as an institution of civic culture that educates students for active citizenship (Aronowitz and Giroux 1993, Sehr 1997, Fraser 1997, Giroux 1997). Situated within a broader context of social responsibility, politics, and the dignity of human life, we must join forces to defend schools as sites that offer students the opportunity to involve themselves in the deepest problems of society. Only then can students acquire the knowledge, skills, and ethical vocabulary necessary for what Havel (1998, 146) has called "the richest possible participation in public life." Educators must defend public schools as indispensable to the life of the nation, because they are one of the few public spaces left where students can learn the power of, and engage in the experience of, democracy.

In the face of increasing corporate takeovers, the ongoing commodification of the curriculum, and the turning of students into consumers, educators must mount a collective struggle to reassert the crucial importance of public education in offering students the skills they need for learning how to govern and take risks. Teachers must help students develop the knowledge necessary for deliberation, reasoned arguments, and social action. At issue is a societal mandate to provide students with an education that allows them to recognize the dream and promise of a substantive democracy—particularly the idea that, as citizens, students are "entitled to public services, decent housing, safety, security, support during hard times, and, most importantly, some power over decision making" (Kelley 1997, 146). Indeed, "the urgency to solve the inequities in schooling is perhaps the most important reason for continuing the struggle to reform public education. For we will not survive as a republic nor move toward a genuine democracy unless we can narrow the gap between the rich and the poor, reduce our racial and ethnic divides, and create a deeper sense of community" (Ascher, Fruchter, and Berne 1996, 112).

More is needed than defending public education as central to developing and nourishing the proper balance between democratic public spheres and commercial power, between identities founded on democratic principles and those steeped in forms of competitive, and self-interested individualism that celebrate their own material and ideological advantages. Given the current assault on educators at all levels of schooling, it is politically crucial that teachers be defended public intellectuals who provide an indispensable service to the nation. Such an appeal cannot be made merely in the name of professionalism; we must instead express it in terms of the civic duty such intellectuals provide. Intellectuals who inhabit public schools represent the conscience of a society because they shape the conditions under which future generations learn about themselves and their relations to others and the world. These teachers also engage pedagogical practices that are moral and political rather than just technical. At its best, these pedagogical practices bear witness to the ethical and political dilemmas animating the broader social landscape.

Organizing against the corporate takeover of schools also suggests fighting to protect collective bargaining and health benefits for teachers, developing legislation to prevent untrained teachers assuming classroom responsibilities, and working to put more power in the hands of faculty members, parents, and students. Public school educators bear the steadily worsening burden, especially in urban centers, of overcrowded classes, limited resources, and hostile legislators.

The corporatizing of U.S. education reflects a crisis of vision regarding the meaning and purpose of democracy at a time when "market cultures, market moralities, market mentalities [are] shattering community, eroding civic society, [and] undermining the nurturing system for children" (West 1994, 42). Yet this crisis also presents a unique opportunity for progressive educators to expand and deepen the meaning of *democracy*—radically defined as a struggle to combine the distribution of wealth, income, and knowledge with recognition and positive valorizing of cultural diversity. They can also reassert the primacy of politics, power, and struggle as a pedagogical task (Fraser 1997). Educators must confront the march of corporate power by resurrecting a noble tradition, extending from Horace Mann to Martin Luther King Jr., that affirms education as a political process encouraging people to identify themselves as more than consuming subjects, and democracy as more than a spectacle of market culture.

Finally, the debate about public education is really about what form the relationship between corporations and public are going to take in the next century. The meaning and purpose of such a debate has not been lost on students. During the first week of March 1998, students from more than 100 colleges held a series of "teach-ins" protesting the intrusion and increasing involvement of corporations in public and higher education (*Chronicle of Higher Education* 1998). For those of us who work in such institutions, it might be the time to take an object lesson from these students and provide an example through our own actions of the meaning and importance of civic courage.

REFERENCES

Aronowitz, S. 1998. "The New Corporate University." *Dollars and Sense* 25 (2): 32–35.

Aronowitz, S., & H. A. Giroux. 1993. *Education Still Under Siege*. Westport, CT: Bergin and Garvey.

Ascher, C., N. Fruchter, & R. Berne. 1996. *Hard Lessons: Public Schools and Privatization*. New York: Twentieth Century Fund Press.

Berliner, D. C., & B. J. Biddle. 1995. *The Manufactured Crisis: Myths, Fraud, and the Attack on America's Public Schools*. Reading, MA: Addison-Wesley.

Bracey, G. 1997. "What Happened to America's Public Schools? Not What You Think?" *American Heritage*, 48 (7): 39–52.

Center for Commercial-Free Public Education. 1998. "Reading, Writing, . . . and Purchasing?" *Educational Leadership* 56 (2): 16.

Chronicle of Higher Education. 1998. "Short Subjects: Students Protest Corporate Influence." *Chronicle of Higher Education* 44 (27): A11.

Consumer Union of the United States. 1995. Captive Kids: A Report on Commercial Pressures on Kids at School. Yonkers, NY: Educational Services. ERIC ED 389 400.

Doyle, D. P. 1994. "The Role of Private Sector Management in Public Education." *Phi Delta Kappan* 76 (2): 128–32.

Finn, C. E., Jr., & D. Kirkpatrick. 1990. *Choice in Schooling: A Case for Tuition Vouchers*. Chicago: Loyola University Press.

Fraser, J. W. 1997. *Reading, Writing, and Justice: School Reform as if Democracy Matters*. Albany: State University of New York Press.

Giroux, H. A. 1997. *Pedagogy and the Politics of Hope: Theory, Culture, and Schooling: A Critical Reader*. Boulder, CO: Westview Press.

Grace, G. 1997. "Politics, Markets, and Democratic Schools." In *Education: Culture, Economy, Society*, edited by A. H. Halsey, H. Lauder, P. Brown, and A. Wells, 311–18. New York: Oxford University Press.

Grossborg, L. 1997. *Bringing It All Back Home: Essays on Cultural Studies*. Durham, NC: Duke University Press.

Havel, V. (trans. P. Wilson). 1998. "The Sad State of the Republic." *The New York Review of Books* 45 (4): 42–46.

Henig, J. 1996. "The Danger of Market Rhetoric." In *Selling Out Our Schools*, edited by R. Lowe and B. Miner, 8–11. Milwaukee: Rethinking Schools Institute.

Herrnstein, R. J., & C. Murray. 1994. *The Bell Curve: Intelligence and Class Structure in American Life*. New York: The Free Press.

Kelley, R. 1997. "Neo-Cons of the Black Nation." *Black Renaissance Noire* 1 (2): 134–46.

Kincheloe, J. L., and S. R. Steinberg, eds. 1997. *Kinderculture: The Corporate Construction of Childhood*. Boulder, CO: Westview Press.

Kozol, J. 1997. "Saving Public Education." *The Nation* (17 February): 16–18.

Labaree, D. F. 1997. "Are Students 'Consumers'? The Rise of Public Education as a Private Good." *Education Week* 17 (3): 48, 38.

Manzo, K. K. 1998. "Calif. School Board Infusing Pedagogy into Frameworks." *Education Week* 17 (20): 7.

Molnar, A. 1996. *Giving Kids the Business: The Commercialization of America's Schools.* Boulder, CO: Westview Press.

Meier, D. W. 1997. "Saving Public Education." *The Nation* (17 February): 23–24.

Perkin, P. 1998. "Schoolhouse Crock: Right-Wing Myths Behind the 'New Stupidity.'" *Extra!* (January/February): 9–10.

Ravitch, D., ed. 1995. *Debating the Future of American Education: Do We Need National Standards and Assessments?* Washington, DC: Brookings Institute.

Sehr, D. T. 1997. *Education for Public Democracy.* Albany: State University of New York Press.

Shapiro, B. 1996. "Privateers Flunk School." *The Nation* (19 February): 4.

Shapiro, S. 1998. "Public School Reform: The Mismeasures of Education." *Tikkun* 13 (1): 51–55.

Stratman, D. 1998. "School Reform and the Attack on Public Education." *Dollars and Sense* 25 (2): 7.

Vine, P. 1997. "To Market, To Market . . . : The School Business Sells Kids Short." *The Nation* (8/15 September): 11–17.

Wechsler, P. 1997. "This Lesson Is Brought To You By . . ." *Business Week* (30 June): 68–69.

West, C. 1994. "America's Three-Fold Crisis." *Tikkun* 9 (2): 41–44.

THE HOLLOW PROMISE OF
SCHOOL VOUCHERS

ROBERT LOWE

For nearly 150 years public education in the United States has been recognized as a fundamental public good. That recognition is now under attack. Building on more than a decade of national power that has radically redefined the nature of public responsibility, conservatives, under the aegis of "choice," have proposed the substitution of markets for public schools. And they have made their arguments plausible to diverse constituencies.

Despite the grave inadequacies of public education today, however, throwing schools open to the marketplace will promote neither excellence nor equality for all. Rather, it will enhance the freedom of the privileged to pursue their advancement unfettered by obligation to community.

Current efforts to promote an educational marketplace through choice trace directly to the work of conservative economist Milton Friedman. Writing in the mid-1950s, Friedman proposed that every family be given a voucher of equal worth for each child attending school. Under this plan, families could choose any school that met rudimentary government oversight (which Friedman likened to the sanitary inspection of a restaurant). Parents could add their own resources to the value of a voucher, and, presumably, schools could set their own tuition level and admission requirements.[1]

At the time, Friedman's proposal failed to attract widespread support. While some people excoriated public schools during the 1950s for curricular laxity that allegedly gave Russians the jump in the space race, optimism prevailed that curriculum innovation and more attention to advanced placement classes would remedy the problem. Further, for the first decade after the 1954 *Brown v. Board of Education* decision, optimism remained high that public schools could create equality of educational opportunity. In fact, it was school desegregation that most underscored the conservative nature of Friedman's stance.

THE FIRST CHOICE PROGRAM

The first choice program provided white students in Virginia public funds to attend private academies in order to avoid attending public schools with Blacks.[2] Friedman addressed this matter in his proposal. Although he expressed his personal desire for integration, he believed that state-imposed desegregation violated parents' freedom to choose. Thus Friedman asserted the primacy of freedom over equality and finessed the lack of freedom the less-than-equal possessed.

During much of the 1960s confidence prevailed that public education could promote both excellence and equity. But by the 1980s such confidence had seriously deteriorated in a political climate that identified the state as the perpetrator rather than the ameliorator of social and economic ills.[3] A wave of national reports contributed to this climate by maintaining that the United States was losing its competitive edge because schools were inadequately developing students' skills.[4] At the same time, sustained inequities in educational outcomes between white students and students of color seriously undermined faith in public schools' capacity to provide equal educational opportunity. In such an environment, a new private school choice program that emphasized opportunities for low-income students of color was linked with a new, more public relations–oriented defense of the educational marketplace. This approach met considerable success in creating the illusion that choice would serve all.

The link was forged publicly in June 1990 when Wisconsin State Rep. Annette "Polly" Williams (D–Milwaukee), the African American sponsor of the highly publicized Milwaukee Parent Choice Program, traveled to Washington, D.C., as a featured participant in the unveiling of *Politics, Markets, and America's Schools* by John Chubb and Terry Moe.[5] Rarely do scholarly works become media events, but this event signified the launching of a vigorous campaign to promote educational choice. It also implied the existence of far broader support for opening schools to the marketplace than the historically conservative constituency for choice would suggest. Although it would be a mistake to conclude that support for "choice" represents a consensus among diverse political forces, it rapidly is becoming the major policy issue affecting schools in the United States today.

To summarize their argument, Chubb and Moe assert that public schools provide inadequate instruction because they lack the autonomy necessary to create effective education; they lack autonomy because they are bureaucratic; and they are bureaucratic because politics shapes them. Thus, they claim the way to create effective schools is to substitute the market for politics. The clarity of their argument and the simplicity of their solution, apparently buttressed by the analysis of massive databases, may seem persuasive. But problems with their formulations abound.

FALSE ASSUMPTIONS

First of all, Chubb and Moe assume that *A Nation at Risk*, along with less influential reports of the 1980s, provides such telling evidence of educational malfeasance that drastic measures are justified.[6] Serious questions might be raised about the test results marshalled to document this state of affairs. It is questionable whether standardized test scores can accurately gauge the nation's educational health, a point Chubb and Moe themselves make in another context.

Even assuming such scores have value, the strategy of *A Nation at Risk* to document both declining scores within the United States and unfavorable comparison of scores with other countries hardly withstands close scrutiny. Its authors fail to note that their data suggest only a modest decline in scores since the 1960s. They do not acknowledge the upward trajectory of scores on several tests in the 1970s and 1980s, and they also ignore tests that showed no decline.[7] Further, the report inappropriately contrasts the achievement of 12th graders in the United States with those of other countries, since the groups are not comparable. Most students in the United States reach the 12th grade, and a high percentage progresses beyond. In many other countries only an elite group completes high school. Thus international comparisons beneath the collegiate level have limited utility.[8]

Lack of evidence indicating "a rising tide of mediocrity," to use the unfortunate phrasing of *A Nation at Risk*, in no way suggests that children of color are receiving an adequate education. But it undercuts the justification of a market-based educational system for all based on the assumption that nothing could be lost by dismantling public schools. More important, Chubb and Moe fail to prove that private schools do a better job than public ones. Scholars have raised a number of questions about the data Chubb and Moe relied upon, including whether a brief multiple-choice test adequately documented student performance and whether the private school sample over-represented elite preparatory schools.[9] Although many Black and Latino families have avoided the degradations of miserable public schools by enrolling their children in Catholic institutions, the mere fact of private status obviously does not confer excellence on schools.

Further, Chubb and Moe exaggerate when they suggest that public schools are rendered incoherent by the variety of political influences that shape them. Their pluralistic notion of educational politics fails to recognize that through most of the twentieth century schools were elite-dominated. Bureaucratic structures, in part, were designed by elites at the turn of the century to remove schools from popular political control.[10] Yet altered power relations can inspire bureaucratic measures that protect the rights of minorities and the poor. Thus recent bureaucratic regulations, engendered by the Civil Rights Movement of the 1960s, are the real objects of conservative complaint. These have promoted desegregation, bilingual education, and education of the handicapped, institutionalizing a modicum of equity in public schools as a response to the demands of those traditionally denied power. That such regulations cannot adequately secure equality of educational opportunity does not mean that the market can do any better.

Chubb and Moe assume that the market will create quality education for everyone through the mechanism of choice. Yet choice certainly has not accomplished this in the private sector of the economy. If the affluent can choose health spas in the Caribbean and gracious homes, the poor must choose inadequate health care and dilapidated housing. To the extent that those with limited resources have won forms of protection, it has not been guaranteed by the play of the market, but by governmental regulation. The conservative agenda of deregulation over the past decade has eroded those protections and greatly increased the disparity between the wealthy and the poor in the United States. A market system of education is merely an extension of deregulation and promises to compound social inequities.

In the market system promoted by Friedman, Chubb and Moe, and conservative political and corporate leaders, public taxation would guarantee relatively modest vouchers worth the same amount for every student in each state. Families, acting as consumers, would then choose the schools their children would attend. But unlike the Milwaukee program where a lottery determines admission, schools may choose as well. Chubb and Moe are adamant about this:

> Schools must be able to define their own missions and build their own programs in their own ways, and they cannot do this if their student population is thrust on them by outsiders. They must be free to admit as many or as few students as they want, based on whatever criteria they think relevant—intelligence, interest, motivation, behavior, special needs—and they must be free to exercise their own, informed judgment about individual applicants.[11]

CHOOSING THE ADVANTAGED

It is in their interest to choose those students who are already high achievers, and it is in their interest—especially for smaller schools—to accept those whose families can supplement the amount of the voucher they are given. Friedman's version of the plan would allow individual families the right to add their own cash to a voucher. Chubb and Moe would allow local districts to augment the value of vouchers through increased local taxation. In either case, the wealthy would have greater choice than the poor.

Advocates of an educational marketplace, then, have won a significant ideological victory by successfully labeling their program "choice" rather than the more neutral sounding "voucher." While no one in their right mind would deny families educational options, "choice" obscures the reality that those who come from economically empowered families are those most likely to be chosen by good schools. As in the marketplace writ large, what one can purchase depends on how much currency is brought to the transaction.

Choice also obscures how the already advantaged would benefit financially at the expense of the less fortunate. A reduced tax
rate would provide the well-to-do with a voucher for part of their
tuition for private schools. This contrasts favorably with the current situation which requires them to pay higher taxes for public
schools in addition to relying solely on their own resources if they
choose private institutions. Such a tax advantage, obvious in the
Friedman plan, would exist in the Chubb and Moe variant as well
since wealthy districts' decisions to raise taxes above the lower
limit would be offset by the abolition of federal and state-level
taxation that redistributes resources to poor districts. For the poor,
in contrast, the baseline vouchers would be difficult to add on to,
creating a situation reminiscent of Southern Jim Crow education
where vast differences existed between per pupil expenditures for
Black and White schools.

Under Jim Crow it was common for African Americans to supplement meager public funding by constructing schoolhouses with
their own donated labor and paying teachers out of their inadequate incomes.[12] But Blacks could not rectify these inequities
despite extraordinary sacrifices. As the scholar W.E.B. DuBois
maintained, if some of these starved schools managed to achieve
excellence through unusual efforts, greater funding would have
made such excellence far more widespread.[13]

A voucher system of education can provide support for
long-established community-based education programs that have
effectively served children of color on shoestring budgets. But as
the failure of the Juanita Virgil Academy suggests, the notion that
choice would create a nation of small, effective schools is a construction as mythical as the notion that the market can maintain a nation of shopkeepers. A high level of capitalization and
economies of scale would be necessary to construct buildings, to
conduct advertising campaigns, to maintain staffing with an un-
predictable number of students, and to make do with the unsup-
plemented vouchers those without wealth would bring. A likely
result would be educational versions of fast-food conglomerates,
with scripted teacher behaviors similar to the standardized patter of
McDonald's order clerks. Like nineteenth century charity schools,
such schools would compose the bottom tier of an educational hierarchy based on privilege.

Aside from the inequities associated with a market-based approach to schooling, such a strategy raises fundamental issues of educational purpose. Should taxpayers contribute to financing schools that have no public accountability no matter how objectionable many might find their goals? Should the public subsidize elite prep schools, schools run for profit, schools with racist ideologies, and schools run by corporations to train future workers? Should families be regarded as entrepreneurial units charged with maximizing their children's educational opportunities? This market ethos ignores any sense of responsibility for other children's education, any obligation for community control of education, any commitment to schools as sites of democratic discourse, any need for the new common curriculum some educators are forging out of the cultural works and political struggles of the diverse peoples who have shaped the United States.

CONSERVATIVES EXACERBATE DIFFERENCES

It is no small irony that so many conservatives have accused the multiculturalist movement of balkanization when their own politics have profoundly exacerbated the real differences that exist between groups in the United States. Certainly Republicans are not solely responsible for a long history of governmental policies that have developed suburban preserves for middle-class whites at the expense of urban economies inhabited by the poor and people of color.[14] Yet since the early 1980s regressive tax reform, diminished social services, and a benign attitude toward the flight of manufacturing jobs beyond U.S. borders have significantly increased the disparity between the wealthy and the poor. Already by 1983, according to historian Robert Weisbrot, "the cumulative impact of Reagan's policies involved a $25 billion transfer in disposable income from the less well-off to the richest fifth of Americans, and a rise in the number of poor people from 29.3 million in 1980 to 35.3 million."[15]

There are now signs that the strategy of suburbanization is yielding to urban gentrification as professional jobs in the service sector replace blue-collar positions. Historian Kenneth Jackson has indicated that rising fuel, land, and housing costs, along with changes in family organization, make suburban living less desirable.[16] In

addition, privatization is a major incentive for the affluent to reset-
tle in cities where inadequate revenues are starving public services.
Increasingly in cities, where deindustrialization and reduced federal
aid have devastated public spaces, urban professionals are paying
only for those services that benefit themselves. These enclaves of
privilege support private country clubs, private security guards, private road repair services, and private schools.[17]

Adding to such services, choice is a way of subsidizing urban
professionals' taste for private education in environments where
even the best public schools do not always accommodate them.
Although virtually every city has magnet schools which disproportionately concentrate school districts' resources on college
preparatory programs for middle-class children, they typically practice at least a rudimentary form of equity that requires some degree of racial balance, and they cannot guarantee admission to all
white middle-class applicants. As choice invites suburbanites back
to the city to enjoy their private pursuits at the expense of reinvigorated public services, they will displace and further marginal-
ize the poor.

In the conservative imagination the divestment of state redistributive functions does not terminate responsibility for the less
fortunate. Rather, such responsibility becomes voluntary, an act
of private choice. Much, in fact, is made of the public spiritedness
of the affluent who voluntarily participate in contributing to the
common good. Enormous publicity, for instance, has attended the
offer of New York businessman Eugene Lang and several others to
guarantee college scholarships to low-income school children, as
well as to provide various supportive academic and counseling
services to see them through high school. Oddly, we hear little
about the federally funded TRIO programs that realized such practices worked decades ago. They have a long record of demonstrated success limited only by funding that is inadequate to reach
more than a small percentage of the eligible population.[18] Massive
federal support of such initiatives, in fact, is paramount because
Lang and a few other philanthropists devoted to equity are exceptions. As [former] U.S. Labor Secretary Robert Reich has pointed
out, the wealthy contribute a lower percentage of their incomes to
charitable purposes than the poor, and what they do give is disproportionately dispensed on elite cultural activities and institu-

tions that serve themselves. Further, Reich notes that the much ballyhooed support of corporations for public schools is less than what they receive in the tax breaks they have successfully won.[19] Choice in giving, like choice in selecting private schools, provides a poor case that private spending will support the public good.

None of this is to say that public schools are beyond reproach. If they adequately served children of color, interest in "choice" would be limited and efforts to secure multicultural education unnecessary. Typically, students in public schools have suffered curricula that are ethnocentric and unquestioningly nationalistic. They also have experienced wide variation in academic quality based on their race and class. Author Jonathan Kozol, for instance, poignantly describes such grave inequities between public schools, underscoring the obvious unfairness of favoring the already advantaged with disproportionate resources.[20] Thus it might make sense to restrict choice programs to the underserved.[21]

OPPOSITION TO AFFIRMATIVE ACTION

This clearly is not what the [former] Bush administration had in mind, however, since it steadfastly opposed affirmative action. Leading Republicans—and conservative groups like the Landmark Legal Center for Civil Rights, which defended the Milwaukee Choice Program in the courts while it opposed the 1990 Civil Rights Act—merely view the Milwaukee program as an opening gambit in an effort to institute vouchers for everyone.[22] This agenda is explicit in a proposal for California initiated by the Excellence Through Choice in Education League. The league's effort to place a statewide measure on the November 1993 ballot mandating vouchers for all was articulated initially as a measure to serve low-income families only.[23]

If public education has inadequately fulfilled its responsibilities to educate all, market-driven educational enterprise cannot fulfill them. At best the popularity of choice among those with the least privilege should send a powerful message to public school educators that the common school for many remains a myth. It highlights the need to support a multicultural agenda that widens public discourse on equity issues and transforms public education in ways that enable people of color to exercise co-ownership of society. Yet the very idea of schools that educate people in common—drawing on the richness of diversity—is antithetical to the intent of the conservative leaders and foundations advocating choice.

Early in the twentieth century corporate elites claimed to take the schools out of politics by creating expert-run centralized and bureaucratic public schools. Their demand for efficiency and impartial expertise masked a politically motivated effort to replace working class influence over education with their own influence. Today Chubb and Moe articulate the position of corporate elites who rail against the bureaucratic schools their predecessors were so influential in creating, once more claiming they want to take schools out of politics. Yet their desire to open them to the marketplace is also an inherently political strategy. It will enable the more affluent to free themselves from the yoke of all the legislative and legal safeguards people have won through the freedom struggles of the 1960s. It furthermore will free the rich from all public educational responsibility, striking a major blow against the current multiculturalist effort that seeks a radical expansion of democracy and a reinvigorated vision of community. The implementation of "choice" would be a victory for narrow class interest over community, accelerating the drastic maldistribution of opportunity that exists today.

NOTES

1. Milton Friedman, "The Role of Government in Education," in Robert A. Solow, ed., *Economics and the Public Interest* (New Brunswick: Rutgers University Press, 1955).

2. The most notorious instance of this occurred in Prince Edward County where public schools were closed for five years. Blacks too were offered vouchers, but, committed to desegregation, they refused and many children received no formal education during that period. See J. Harvie Wilkinson III, *From Brown to Bakke: The Supreme Court and School Integration, 1954–1978* (New York: Oxford University Press, 1979), pp. 98–100.

3. See Charles Murray, *Losing Ground: American Social Policy, 1950–1980* (New York: Basic Books, 1984); Diane Ravitch, *The Troubled Crusade: American Education, 1945–1980* (New York: Basic Books, 1983).

4. See especially National Commission on Excellence in Education, *A Nation at Risk: The Imperative for Educational Reform* (Washington, DC: Government Printing Office, 1983).

5. John E. Chubb and Terry M. Moe, *Politics, Markets and America's Schools* (Washington, DC: The Brookings Institution, 1990).

6. NCEE, *A Nation at Risk.*

7. See Lawrence C. Stedman and Carl F. Kaestle, "The Test Score Decline Is Over: Now What?" *Phi Delta Kappan* (November 1985), pp. 204–10; Lawrence C. Stedman and Marshall S. Smith, "Weak Arguments, Poor Data, Simplistic Recommendations," in Beatrice and Ronald Gross, eds., *The Great School Debate* (New York: Touchstone, 1985), pp. 83–105.

8. Stedman and Smith, p. 90.

9. See, for example, Peter H. Rossi and James D. Wright, "Best Schools—Better Discipline or Better Students? A Review of High School Achievement," *American Journal of Education* 91 (November 1982), p. 82; comments on John Witte's unpublished paper presented at 1990 meeting of American Political Science Association, *Education Week* (November 14, 1990), p. 20.

10. David Tyack, *The One Best System: A History of American Urban Education* (Cambridge, MA: Harvard University Press, 1976), pp. 132–33.

11. Chubb and Moe, pp. 221–22.

12. James Anderson, *The Education of Blacks in the South, 1861 to 1935* (Chapel Hill: University of North Carolina Press, 1988).

13. W.E.B. DuBois, "Pechstein and Pechsniff." *The Crisis* 36 (September 1929), p. 314.

14. Policies have included federal highway subsidies, segregationist FHA loans, zoning ordinances, and legal standing for restrictive covenants. See Kenneth T. Jackson, *Crabgrass Frontier: The Suburbanization of the United States* (New York: Oxford University Press, 1985), p. 293; Ira Katznelson and Margaret Weir, *Schooling for All: Class, Race and the Decline of the Democratic Ideal* (Berkeley: University of California Press, 1985), p. 217.

15. Robert Weisbrot, *Freedom Bound: A History of America's Civil Rights Movement* (New York: Plume, 1991), p. 302.

16. Jackson, *Crabgrass Frontier,* pp. 297–303.

17. See, for instance, Robert B. Reich, "Secession of the Successful," *The New York Times Magazine* (January 20, 1991), p. 42.

18. See *Chronicle of Higher Education* (July 3, 1991), p. A17.

19. Reich, "Secession of the Successful," pp. 43, 44.

20. Jonathan Kozol, *Savage Inequalities: Children in America's Schools* (New York: Crown Publishers, 1991).

21. For advocacy of choice programs with redistributive goals, see John E. Coons and Stephen D. Sugarman, *Education by Choice: The Case for Family Control* (Berkeley: University of California Press, 1978), p. 31; Henry M. Levin, "Educational Choice and the Pains of Democracy," in Thomas James and Henry M. Levin, eds., *Public Dollars for Private Schools* (Philadelphia: Temple University Press, 1983), pp. 36–37.

22. The Landmark Legal Center is funded in part by the Bradley Foundation *Milwaukee Journal* (July 23, 1990), pp. 1, 4; for its opposition to the 1990 Civil Rights Act, see *New York Times* (October 21, 1990), p. 15.

23. *Education Week* (September 18, 1991), p. 1.

FOR-PROFITS TARGET EDUCATION

BARBARA MINER

In September 1990, *Good Morning America* was broadcast from South Pointe Elementary School in Dade County, FL. The news peg? It was the first day of school in what was to be a new and glorious era in education: for-profit, private companies running public schools.

South Pointe was run by the for-profit Education Alternatives, Inc. (EAI), which was the first for-profit private firm under contract to run a public school, and which at the time was the darling of the privatization movement.

John Golle, head of EAI, boasted that his company could run public schools for the same amount of money, improve achievement, and still make a profit. "There's so much fat in the schools that even a blind man without his cane would find the way," he told *Forbes* magazine in 1992.

EAI's rhetoric never matched its educational and financial reality, however. EAI soon found it couldn't run public schools for less than the districts it contracted with, and its promises of academic improvement proved elusive.

By the spring of 2000, EAI was in the midst of a corporate and educational meltdown. The company, which has changed its name to Tesseract Group Inc., was millions in debt, kicked off Nasdaq when its stock price tumbled to pennies a share, and couldn't even afford the postage to mail report cards home to parents at one of its remaining charter schools in Arizona. Today, the company is in bankruptcy.

The tale of EAI is more than historical anecdote, however. It provides interesting parallels to the problems facing one of the hottest trends in education: the move by for-profit companies to run public schools.

The biggest controversy currently centers on Philadelphia, where the for-profit Edison Schools is attempting to secure a six-year, $101 million consulting contract and a separate deal to run as many as 45 of the 60 district schools due to be privatized as "partnership schools." Edison has the backing of Gov. Mark Schweiker, a Republican, who pushed through a plan this December to allow the state's takeover of the district. But it has run into stiff and ongoing community resistance.

"What has turned many in the community against Edison is not only that the company's sweeping claims of success do not stand up to scrutiny," notes Paul Socolar, editor of the grassroots *Philadelphia Public School Notebook*, "but also that Edison intends to extract a large profit from a school district that is already profoundly underfunded."

Overall, more than 22 businesses, groups, and institutions have applied to run one or more of the 60 "partnership schools." For-profit contenders include Chancellor Beacon Academies of Miami, Charter Schools USA of Fort Lauderdale, FL, and Mosaica Education Inc. of San Rafael, CA. A variety of non-profit groups such as Temple University are also seeking to run partnership schools.

WHAT IS PRIVATIZATION?

Privatization, while couched in rhetoric extolling the ability of the marketplace to unleash creativity and innovation, at heart is a way for for-profit companies to get their hands on a bigger share of the $350 billion K–12 education industry. On Wall Street, privatization has one single focus: Can for-profit education management companies make a profit?

The verdict is decidedly still out on that matter. While some privately held companies report profits, there is not a single for-profit, publicly held educational management company that has shown an ongoing ability to make money. Edison, the biggest and most important for-profit firm, has lost more than $233.5 million in the last decade.

Yet the controversy goes beyond whether private companies can eke out profits from already underfunded school districts. Privatization inherently leads to private control; it undercuts democratic oversight and decision-making of what is a public institution—and turns such control over to private forces focused on making money, not on doing what is in the best interests of children and society at large.

Private sector involvement in public education is not a new phenomenon. For decades, public schools have purchased any number of products and services from private companies—whether textbook companies or bus companies providing transportation.

But in the last decade, privatization took on a new meaning as for-profit companies hoped to get involved in education at a higher and qualitatively different level. Their goal: to run entire schools or entire districts—from the hiring of teachers to the development of curriculum to the teaching of students. In the process, they plan to "compete" with publicly run schools and redefine the very definition of public education—transforming it from a public service into a source of private profit.

The Wall Street term for such companies is Educational Management Organizations (EMOS). And if you like HMOs, as many on Wall Street do, you'll love EMOs. Investors, in fact, are fond of comparing public education to the healthcare industry of 25 years ago, before the nationwide ascendancy of HMOs.

"Education today, like health care 30 years ago, is a vast, highly localized industry ripe for change," Mary Tanner, managing director of Lehman Brothers, said, at a 1996 Education Industry Conference in New York City. "The emergence of HMOs and hospital management companies created enormous opportunities for investors. We believe the same pattern will occur in education."

In the last year, there has been a consolidation within the for-profit school management companies, reducing the number of key players. Those remaining:

Edison Schools Inc. Formed in 1992 and based in New York City, Edison is by far the biggest and most important player in the field. It currently runs 136 schools serving 75,000 students, in 22 states and the District of Columbia. In July, in an example of the industry consolidation, Edison acquired the privately held LearnNow. Edison is the only publicly held company among the major for-profit education management companies. Key investors have included Microsoft founder Paul Allen ($71 million through his Vulcan Ventures in 1999), J.P. Morgan Chase & Co., and Investor AB, a Swedish holding company.

Contracts representing more than 30 percent of Edison's revenue will expire by the end of the 2002–2003 school year, which is one reason the Philadelphia deal is crucial to Edison. In the short term, such a contract would bolster the stockholder confidence needed to keep stock prices from plummeting. (Edison went public in November 1999 at a starting price of about $18 a share. In the beginning of 2002, its stock was basically flat, selling between $17 and $19 a share, and in mid-February it was down to about $14 a share.)

Chancellor Beacon Academies, formed by the merger in January 2002 of Beacon Education Management of Westborough, Massachusetts and Miami-based Chancellor Academies, Inc. The new company, the second largest for-profit school management company in the United States, serves about 19,000 students on 46 campuses in eight states and the District of Columbia.

Mosaica Education Inc., of San Rafael, CA. Mosaica is running 22 schools this year in 11 states; in June, it took over the struggling Advantage Schools Inc.

National Heritage Academies, Grand Rapids, MI. National Heritage, with 28 schools in 2001–2002, operates mostly in Michigan and North Carolina. It emphasizes moral values and character education in a setting that opponents claim is thinly veiled religious education.

Many investors speak bullishly of Edison and the other for-profit school management companies. Michigan industrialist J. C. Huizenga, who has invested more than $50 million in National Heritage Academics, characterized for-profit education this way to *Business Week* last year, "This is a breakthrough business opportunity."

Others are more cautious. Allen Greenberg, editor of the *Philadelphia Business Journal*, wrote this fall, "I took at look at some of Edison's recent filings with the Securities and Exchange Commission. It's not a pretty picture." His bottom-line analysis: that Edison's financials "should give even the most ardent supporters of privatization cause to go slow."

Even Edison has been forced to bluntly acknowledge its unprofitability. In filings with the Securities and Exchange Commission (SEC), Edison has repeatedly noted, "We have not yet demonstrated that public schools can be profitably managed by private companies and we are not certain when we will become profitable, if at all."

TOUGH SLEDDING FOR EDISON

In several high-profile districts, it has not been a good year for Edison's image. For example:

> In New York City, last spring, the company lost a community/ parental vote on whether the company should manage five New York schools. The vote was doubly embarrassing because it came in a city where Edison is headquartered, and because it was the parents who rejected Edison. (This is the only instance where Edison's future has been decided by the votes of parents, not politicians.)

> In Wichita, KS, the school board voted unanimously on Jan. 28 to take back two of Edison's four schools in the district— Edison-Ingalls and Edison-Isely elementary. At Ingalls, enrollment dropped from a high of 722 in 1997 to 426 this year, while more than half of the teaching staff left after the end of the last school year. At Isely, enrollment dropped from about 280 to 200.

> Edison says the teachers left because they did not like the company's longer school year. But a number of teachers from Ingalls told *The Wichita Eagle* that they were driven out by intolerable working conditions. "The work environment was horrifically hostile," said teacher Jeanette Falley. In addition, the school's principal and assistant principal were removed last December after it was found that school personnel improperly helped students on standardized tests.

> In Dallas, the school board forced Edison to renegotiate its five-year contract when it was found that Edison would have other wise received $20 million more than the actual cost of running its seven schools.

> In San Francisco, parents and school board members revoked Edison's charter when test scores showed that the school's

performance was the absolute worst among the city's schools. Under political pressure, the state stepped in and granted Edison an independent charter so the school could keep going.

The San Francisco battle also highlighted issues of whether Edison has genuine parental support, after it hired a professional organizing and marketing company, Digital Campaigns, to generate support among parents. Digital Campaigns, for example, boasted on its website that Edison was able to attract only five parent signatures on a petition until Digital Campaigns stepped in to help. Caroline Grannan, a San Francisco public school parent and co-founder of Parents Advocating School Accountability, says, "It's impossible to know how many 'happy parents' would be speaking up without the professional organizing operation."

BETTER TEST SCORES

One of the biggest controversies in all of the districts where it operates involves whether Edison's schools actually perform better than public schools. Edison says yes, but the company's performance indicates otherwise. And not just in San Francisco.

Dallas Superintendent Mike Moses told *The American School Board Journal* this December that "we looked at their seven schools against seven comparable schools, and truthfully, Edison's performance was not superior."

Gerald Bracey, author of *The War Against America's Public Schools*, issued a report in early February on Edison's claims of improved academic achievement, and said that Edison makes "hyperbolic conclusions, using data that can only be described as questionable."

A recent study of 10 Edison schools by the National Education Association, done by the Evaluation Center at Western Michigan University researcher Gary Miron, found that Edison schools are performing the same as or slightly worse overall than comparable public schools. "Our findings suggest that Edison students do not perform as well as Edison claims in its annual reports," the report said. An earlier report by the American Federation of Teachers reached similar conclusions.

U.S. Rep. Chaka Fattah (D–PA) reviewed Edison's claims of improved achievement this fall and found that "the overwhelming majority of Edison schools perform poorly, and in many cases are fairing worst than some Philadelphia schools."

Edison disputes such reports as political sniping. The RAND Corp., a respected independent research group, has been hired by Edison to analyze the company's academic achievement, but the report will not be completed until 2003 or 2004.

WHY TURN TO PRIVATIZATION

Given the concerns around privatization, why would a school district contract with a for-profit company?

At least in part, the answer lies in the intensive lobbying and political connections of privatization advocates. While there may be doubts about the educational value of privatization, the movement has the support of well-heeled investors with strong ties to political powerbrokers.

Another part of the answer lies in the belief that there are quick fixes that will improve schools, especially in underfunded urban districts. School districts are sometimes open to privatization because officials are tired of fighting taxpayers and state legislators for the increased money they know is essential to get the job done, and are equally tired of being blamed for failures they believe are beyond their control.

Finally, the power of the school privatization movement cannot be separated from the growing clout of market ideology not only in the United States but around the world. As "globalization" becomes not just a market strategy but an increasingly dominant worldview, the very concept of institutions designed to serve the public good rather than generate money for stockholders is seen as hopelessly idealistic and anachronistic.

WHO WINS, WHO LOSES?

Ultimately, for-profit firms will not live or die on their educational record but on their ability to generate profits. And so far, that record is dismal. In the long run, the problem facing Edison is the same that faced the now bankrupt Tesseract, formerly known as EAI. Despite perceptions, there is little "fat" in urban public school

budgets. Nor are there any "silver bullets" that will magically improve schools.

Because education is a labor-intensive industry, there are only
two ways to make money: cut wages or cut services. (A variation
on "cut wages" is hiring younger, lower-paid staff. A variation on
"cut services" is controlling student admissions so that more-
difficult-to-educate students are discouraged.) Like Tesseract, Edison has been plagued by charges that it saves money by hiring
less-experienced teachers and that it doesn't adequately serve special education students.

And when Edison announced this fall that its plan for Philadelphia included cutting the costs of support staff, it was following a
pattern established by EAI. When EAI went into its first multi-
school contract in Baltimore in 1992, one of the first things it did
was replace $10-an-hour, unionized paraprofessional workers with
$7-an-hour "interns" who did not have benefits.

That doesn't mean, however, that some people didn't make a
lot of money off of EAI. Likewise, some people are in line to make
millions off of Edison.

For example, EAI founder and CEO Golle, ever the shrewd businessman, knew when to make his move. In the fall of 1993, over a
two-month period when EAI stock was riding high, Golle took advantage of stock options to make a net gain of approximately $1.75
million on sales of 50,000 shares of EAI common stock.

Edison founder Chris Whittle has likewise been smart enough
to play the stock option game. In one day alone last March, some
650,000 shares held indirectly by Whittle were sold for more than
$15 million. According to a proxy statement filed this fall, Whit-
tle still owns 3.7 million shares of Edison's publicly traded stock,
and he and his associates have options on an additional 4.4 million shares of Edison's publicly traded stock.

To cite a few other examples. Schmidt made more than
$400,000 in Edison stock sales in 2001, on top of his six-figure
salary. Christopher Cerf, Chief Operating Officer for Edison, made
$880,000 in Edison stock sales in 2001, while Jeffrey Leeds, a di-
rector in Edison, made more then $2 million off Edison stock sales
last year. On June 12, Vice-President Deborah McGriff (wife of
voucher and privatization proponent Howard Fuller) sold 15,325

shares of the roughly 200,000 stock options she held when the company first went public—for a gain of $348,184.

But, as Enron demonstrates, lots of questionable companies can win influential friends. The for-profit education privatization movement is not likely to go away just because the companies are not yet making profits. A lot of people with a lot of money are in this for the long run.

Nonetheless, advocates of improved schools shouldn't be fooled that privatization is somehow about education reform. In the end, power and money—who gets more and who gets less—remains at the heart of the privatization struggle. Educational improvement is a sideshow.

"CHOICE" AND OTHER WHITE LIES

MAKANI N. THEMBA

In 1966, at six years old, I was one of six Black children in a bus-ing "experiment" to "integrate" an all-white elementary school in Queens, New York City. Far above the Mason-Dixon Line, my parents thought I would be safe from the savage anti-integration sentiment they saw in Little Rock, AK or Jackson, MI.

Boy, were they wrong.

Every day, the six of us would anxiously touch hands as we took the early morning ride from Hollis, in southern Queens, to the northern community of Little Neck. Hollis was a newly Black and middle-class community back then—made newly Black by the hurried panic of whites moving to places like Little Neck, where they thought they'd be "safe."

Our coming made them feel unsafe. And we were not prepared for the their violence—and hatred.

Teachers, students, and parents taunted us constantly. Students were given special dispensation not to hold our hands or in any way have contact. After a day of abuse in school, we would leave school as we entered—dodging rocks and epithets. The rocks never hit anyone. The epithets did. They hit and burrowed deep into our souls.

This is how the "choice" movement began—with the rock throwers and the naysayers. It was, and is, a movement rooted in fear. It was, and is, a movement that flees from public education rather than fights for public schools that serve all children, regard-less of color or income.

It is no coincidence that this country's first school voucher movement gave public dollars to white students in Virginia to at-tend private, segregated schools following the 1954 *Brown vs. Board of Education* decision legally banning racially separate and unequal education.

At the time, conservatives were in the forefront of opposing the Supreme Court decision. Today, conservatives are once again taking a strong interest in school vouchers—only this time in the guise of concern for Black folk.

Aided by millions in funding from conservative think tanks and public relations firms, today's voucher movement has a much slicker image. And it is attracting diverse faces.

A high profile, big-ticket ad campaign is pushing the idea of school vouchers in the African-American community, although the campaign uses the more appealing term "choice." The ads— and their backers—are part of the complex relationship of school reform to race.

The television and radio ads, sponsored by the Black Alliance for Educational Options (BAEO),[1] are numerous, plaintive, and compelling. Black folk. Regular. Sincere. Speaking directly about their aspirations for their children's education and lives.

Given prevailing stereotypes of Black apathy and neglect, the ads would be right on target if it weren't for the group's solution: school vouchers.

While the ads target the Black community, the white conservatives bankrolling and controlling the school voucher movement have a far broader agenda. Instead of providing the money needed to improve public schools, they want to use public tax dollars for vouchers for private schools. Since most voucher plans do not approach the cost of tuition at the best private schools, it's clear that in the long run, vouchers are a way to help the (mostly white) well-to-do flee public schools. The overwhelming majority of students of color, meanwhile, will remain in even more poorly-funded public schools.

The difference between the "choice" movement and authentic school reform is the difference between abandonment and accountability. Vouchers enable parents to withdraw public education dollars and spend them at private schools. It is the ultimate breach in the social contract. Taxpayers are no longer a community unit committed to maintaining public education for all. They are individual consumers out for the best deal.

At the heart of the *Brown vs. Board* decision was its understanding of the relationship of race to resources and educational quality.

---

[1]Contributors to the BAEO include prominent conservative organizations such as the Lynde and Harry Bradley Foundation, the Walton Family Foundation, and Milton and Rose D. Friedman Foundation.

Yet conservative groups downplay the importance of funding. A case in point: one BAEO press release touts research that it's "choice"—not books, good teachers, and a rigorous curriculum—that advances Black education.

According to the BAEO, the only choice that matters is choosing a better school over a struggling school. But this sidesteps the underlying problem: that the bad schools are concentrated in Black and Brown communities. We need to fight to improve the entire system, not for a better place within it for select individuals.

This is not to deny that many schools are in trouble. But the answer lies in wholesale reform, not in a few of us taking the money and running.

But the conservatives are not interested in real reform because it costs too much money.

Clearly, money matters. Who gets it and for what purpose is at the heart of the education debate.

These are debates and decisions that have been fraught with racism, controversy, and even intrigue for centuries. School vouchers are no different.

BLACK–WHITE INEQUALITY

Inequitable funding and the resulting low-quality schools stem from yet another broken promise of Reconstruction.

After the Civil War, Blacks fought for access to the nation's "great equalizer," public education, as part of the tremendous debt owed us. The debt concerning education is a literal one. Under slavery, in a practice that continued with "indentured" children in post slavery years, it was common for Black children to be "loaned" out as apprentices in exchange for cash to support the private school tuition of their "owner's" children. In other words, for at least three centuries white children of the gentry were educated as a direct result of wages provided by Black children who were deprived of education.[2]

[2]See *Neglected Stories: The Constitution and Family Values*, Peggy Cooper Davis (Hill and Wang, 1997); or *American Negro Slave Revolts*, Herbert Aptheker (International Publishers, 1983).

The right of Blacks to quality education was an important part of the struggle during Reconstruction. In fact, African Americans led the fight for free public schools for all, and working in alliance with whites brought such a victory to the South for the first time.

The 1954 *Brown vs. Board* decision came after almost a century of sustained organizing and agitation. Many thought that *Brown* would force an equitable division of resources and end the separate and unequal schooling that was the hallmark of U.S. education. But whites rebelled. When all else failed, they moved out of cities with any significant Black population, thereby accelerating the march toward sprawl and suburbanity. They even started their own private schools to avoid contact with Blacks.

This is the true beginning of the "choice" movement.

It's a fascinating transition that "choice," used to support segregation and white flight, is now allegedly designed to help Black children.

It's not the first time that conservatives have changed their tune in order to advance their interests. Just a century ago, these same interests were working to ban private schooling and make public schools mandatory. They introduced state laws designed to outlaw Catholic schools (for the Irish), Hebrew schools, and German schools organized by the many immigrant families trying to hold on to their heritage on these shores. The Ku Klux Klan was a major advocate of these mandatory public school attendance laws. They were concerned that children in private schools would be taught "foreign values" that would pose a threat to the "American way of life."

FRIGHT AND FLIGHT

With the advent of school integration, it is now public schools that are the "threat." Fear of attending school with people of color and concerns over issues, such as sex education and multicultural curricula are driving even more white families to private schools or home schooling. It's impossible to understand the voucher movement without looking at this broader context.

The conservatives pushing school vouchers are not committed to fighting for better schools for all. They are seeking to pull much-needed resources out of public schools and funnel the money into private schools. Fundamentally, they are looking for new ways for whites to maintain segregation and privilege. (Nationwide, 78 percent of private school students are white; 9 percent are African American and 8 percent are Latino.)

In order to keep white families in public schools following de-segregation mandates, magnet schools and in school academies became especially popular. Tracking has also been used to maintain separate and unequal schooling, even in nominally integrated schools. A recent study by the Applied Research Center "No Exit? Testing, Tracking, and Students of Color in U.S. Public Schools," (http://www.arc.org), found that tracking is most common in schools with significant numbers of African American and/or Latino students. Further, white students—regardless of test scores, grades or behavior—are much more likely to be placed in "higher tracks" or academic programs.

COLLEGE ADMISSIONS

Perhaps the best example of the conservative movement's unabashed commitment to white privilege is found in its efforts at the post-secondary level.

As high-paying factory jobs of the industrial economy disappear, a college education is now critical to ensure a life without poverty. As a result, college admissions, especially at the graduate level, have become highly competitive.

In recent years, there has been a proliferation of lawsuits and policies at both the state and federal level designed to limit access to college (especially graduate school) for students of color, and to expand access for whites. Special outreach measures like affirmative action have been under growing attack. The clearest example is California, where a 1996 ballot measure curtailed the ability of colleges and universities to consider racial diversity as part of their hiring and admissions criteria.

At the same time, whites are suing for race-conscious admissions to gain unprecedented access to historically Black colleges and universities so that they have expanded options for college education. For example, Alabama State University is currently operating under a 1995 federal court ruling by District Judge Harold L. Murphy, requiring that it set aside nearly 40% of its academic grants budget for scholarships to whites. The state augments the university's $229,000 contribution with public funds, bringing the "whites only" scholarship fund to $1 million a year. Until recently, a white student applying for such a scholarship needed only a "C" average. African Americans vying for admission to the university, meanwhile, had to earn almost a full point higher to even merit consideration. (According to recent press articles, the university has raised the grade point average required for white scholarships, partly in response to a current lawsuit by an African-American student.)

Aside from the irony of such a policy that cuts off African Americans from institutions established to help address the deep inequalities of slavery and its aftermath, there are no accompanying requirements for historically white colleges and universities. On the contrary, affirmative action efforts to integrate such historically white universities are under attack.

BACK TO THE FUTURE

After centuries of fighting for equal education, more and more African Americans are understandably weary. For those who can afford to augment vouchers and get their kids into a great private school, vouchers might sound like a good idea. But for the rest of us, vouchers undermine the ability of African-American kids to get an education at all, because they further defund the public schools where the overwhelming majority of our kids will remain.

Vouchers also divert resources and responsibility from the public sector and move them all to the market. It's all about getting the money, yet without any accountability.

In the days of the historic *Brown* case, many Black people put their lives on the line in the fight for quality public schools for all. This was the real choice movement. It wasn't about slick ad campaigns. It was a movement that took place in the basements of churches and at the kitchen tables of mamas and grandmas who cared deeply for all their communities' children.

The new choice movement, with its clandestine commitment to advancing white privilege and its crass consumer approach to education, is a betrayal of this legacy.

SCHOOL CHOICE CRUCIBLE
A Case Study of Boulder Valley

KENNETH HOWE, MARGARET EISENHART,
AND DAMIAN BETEBENNER

School choice is a controversial public education reform—but not as controversial as it should be. Support for choice remains strong in the face of mounting evidence that long-standing controversies are being decided in favor of the critics of choice. Our study of the choice program in the Boulder Valley School District adds to the growing body of research documenting serious flaws in the theory, procedures, and outcomes of school choice.

Advocates of school choice contend that competition gives parents a voice and the power to vote with their feet. Schools that consistently perform poorly will lose "clients" and be forced to go "out of business," resulting in overall improvement in both achievement and parental satisfaction. Advocates of choice also contend that school choice can better accommodate a diversity of student interests and needs than the "one-size-fits-all" approach they ascribe to traditional public schools. Finally, they contend that school choice can reduce inequities. School choice is really nothing new, according to them, for parents have long chosen schools by choosing their place of residence. A choice policy that removes attendance boundaries permits students to attend schools independent of the price of houses in the neighborhoods in which they live and of their parents' power to influence school officials. It thus provides all parents with choice and so promises to promote diversity in schools.

Critics respond that competition for enrollment destroys cooperation among teachers, schools, and communities and that it provides no answer to the question of what to do with the students who are being harmed while schools are declining, before they "go out of business." Instead of increasing achievement overall, competition only stratifies school achievement, as certain schools use exclusive admissions procedures or tout the high test scores of their students in order to "skim" the most able students. Regarding student interests and needs, critics contend that genuinely public schools must be open to all students. Choice schools exclude difficult-to-teach students and force other public schools to carry an unfair burden. Finally, critics argue that school choice is much more likely to exacerbate inequity than to mitigate it. Without free transportation and adequate information, which public choice plans typically fail to provide, many parents will be unable to exercise choice. Schools will also be subjected to unfair comparisons, for they will be judged in terms of the same criteria, especially test scores, with no regard for the kinds of students they enroll or the resources they can garner.

These claims and counterclaims—about competition, meeting student needs, and equity—provided the general framework that we brought to bear on our study of the Boulder Valley School District's "open enrollment" system. We revisit them below in some detail.

SETTING FOR THE STUDY

Boulder Valley School District (BVSD) is centered in Boulder, Colorado. Boulder has a population of 96,000. It is home to the main campus of the University of Colorado and is ringed by high-tech corporations such as IBM, Sun Microsystems, Ball Aerospace, and Storage Tek. The median household income in Boulder is $51,000, and the city's residents are highly educated. Nearly 30% of the adult population holds graduate or professional degrees. Boulder is noted for its left leaning politics in an otherwise conservative state, so much so that it has been nicknamed "The People's Republic."

Boulder Valley School District reaches well beyond the confines of the city of Boulder. In the western reaches of the district are the sparsely populated foothills of the Rocky Mountains. The vast majority of students from this region are white. In the eastern reaches, particularly in the town of Lafayette, the largest concentration of minorities is located; they are predominantly Latino. Within the city of Boulder, the northern section is older and has a relatively high proportion of minorities, also predominantly Latino. The southern section is newer and has few minorities.

Central Boulder is relatively old, like North Boulder, but the demographics of the public school students more closely resemble those of South Boulder.

School choice has existed in the BVSD since 1961. However, it did not become a significant practice and source of controversy until the mid-1990s. Spurred by parents who were unhappy with the district's implementation of the "middle school philosophy" or who complained about a perceived lack of emphasis on academics in BVSD more generally, various choice options began to proliferate. Coincident with these developments, a new school board sympathetic to choice was elected, and the superintendent responsible for the middle school philosophy was pressured to resign. This was also a time when the school choice movement began accelerating at both state and national levels.

As open enrollment expanded in BVSD, four choice options were added to the traditional option of enrolling in any neighborhood school on a space-available basis: 1) *focus schools*, which offer a particular curricular focus; 2) *neighborhood focus schools*, which give priority to students from within the neighborhood attendance area; 3) *strand schools*, which offer the standard BVSD curriculum alongside a different curricular strand; and 4) *charter schools*, whose accountability to BVSD is specified in a contract.

In 1999–2000, 21 of 57 BVSD schools had incorporated one of the types of choice options described above: one of two K–8 schools, 11 of 33 elementary schools, five of 13 middle schools, and four of nine high schools. To put this in historical perspective, prior to the 1994–95 school year, there were five articulated choice options in BVSD, all emphasizing diversity, experiential learning, integrated learning, or bilingual education, sometimes in combination. Between 1994–95 and 1999–2000, 16 new articulated choice options were added, half of which adopted the "new mission" of an explicit emphasis on academic rigor and college preparation. Core Knowledge was most prominent among the new options provided; five schools adopted it.

More than 20% of students now take advantage of open enrollment to attend BVSD schools other than those assigned to them by attendance area—an unusually high percentage.[1] And whereas the effects of school choice are typically hard to pin down[2] BVSD is a relatively closed system. Thus it provides the opportunity to examine the gains *and* losses among schools when all must compete for enrollment from the same pool of students. It is a school choice crucible.

THE STUDY DATA

We collected data from five sources: 1) surveys of parents and educators in BVSD schools; 2) focus group discussions with this same group; 3) a follow-up survey of principals; 4) a random telephone survey of BVSD parents; and 5) statistical records on open enrollment, test scores, demographics, funding, and fund-raising.

The BVSD Department of Research and Evaluation supplied most of the statistical records. Some of these data spanned the school years from 1994–95 to 2000–2001, and some were limited to 1998–99 and 1999–2000. Fifty-five of the 57 schools in the school district were included in the analyses based on statistical records.

The parent/educator surveys (hereafter called "school surveys") and focus group discussions were designed to determine what people who are actively involved in BVSD schools believe about choice. The participants were 466 individuals representing 43 "schools" (we consider strands and focus schools sharing sites to be separate schools). All but three choice schools, counting strands, were included. A sample of neighborhood schools was selected geographically to include several from each of the district's eight regions. The overall sample contained 23 neighborhood schools, 16 "choice schools," and four "bilingual choice schools." There were five high schools, 11 middle schools, and 28 elementary schools (K–8 schools were counted as both elementary and middle).

Participants in the school surveys and the focus groups were on the "School Improvement Teams," which typically included the principal, teachers, and parents. The sample was disproportionately white, highly educated, and female, reflecting the characteristics of the people most active in BVSD school communities.

The telephone surveys were designed to elicit the beliefs of district parents who had not participated in choice and were not active in schools. Eighty-five potential respondents from each of eight geographic regions were selected at random. Potential respondents were called until 30 completed surveys were obtained from each region, yielding a total of 240 telephone surveys. This sample was more representative of parents in BVSD than were the school surveys, except for including a disproportionate number of women.

Data from the five sources were combined and analyzed, as appropriate, to address three general issues: parents' and educators' perceptions of open enrollment, patterns associated with open enrollment and the factors contributing to them, and funding and fund-raising.

PARENTS' AND EDUCATORS' PERCEPTIONS OF OPEN ENROLLMENT

In general, BVSD parents, teachers, and staff members believe that their schools should focus primarily on the development of social, citizenship, and academic skills in safe, comfortable environments in which teachers are sensitive to student needs. Most parents said that they chose their children's schools on the basis of their curricula, teachers, and staff and that they found these factors to be the major strengths of their particular schools. There was very strong, nearly unanimous agreement that school choice is an effective means of responding to the diversity of students' interests and needs.

Agreement was equally strong that inequities exist in the choice system. For example, almost all agreed that lack of transportation and information reduced or eliminated the opportunities for certain parents to participate in choice. But people were divided on the scope, seriousness, and cause of inequities. People in the neighborhood schools, and to a lesser extent in the bilingual choice schools, tended to see the exacerbation of inequities associated with skimming, stratification by race and income ("white flight"), and unequal resources as serious and direct outcomes of the expansion of choice. A number of individuals in this group also voiced complaints about unfair competition between neighborhood and choice schools and about how the requirement to market their schools diverted resources and efforts from the educational missions of their schools.

By contrast, people in the "new mission" choice schools had few concerns about unfair competition or the market imperative.

They touted their high parental satisfaction ratings and saw "new mission" schools as raising achievement in the district overall. They also tended to see the claims about skimming and "white flight" as overblown or to attribute those phenomena to causes other than the expansion of choice, such as demographic shifts within the district.

The weight of the evidence from our study is not on the side of proponents of "new mission" schools. Although market competition seems to be "working" in the sense that the schools with the highest test scores are most in demand and are those with which parents are most satisfied, concerns about the inequities associated with skimming, stratification, unfair competition, and unequal resources proved well founded.

PATTERNS ASSOCIATED WITH OPEN ENROLLMENT

Our study looked at a number of patterns that emerged in the open-enrollment system and tried to determine the factors that contributed to them.

Demand for BVSD Schools

Two factors were most strongly associated with "demand" (the number of open enrollment requests for a school corrected for its size): test scores and parental satisfaction. Latinos, however, were less motivated by test scores and satisfaction ratings than were whites, or they were willing to overlook those factors in electing bilingual programs.

Based on annual BVSD surveys, parents were more satisfied with choice schools than with neighborhood schools, and they were most satisfied with "new mission" schools. It is reasonable to infer that giving parents a greater voice in the operation of schools and the power to choose the curricula and methods of instruction they deem best for their children can explain much of this attitude. On the other hand, this is not the whole explanation, for parental satisfaction was highly associated with test scores, and the test scores of choice schools tended to be the highest.

Skimming

The emphasis on test scores was reflected in the pools of students who requested open enrollment for sixth and ninth grades, the entry grades for middle school and high school. In general, the students requesting open enrollment had higher test scores than their BVSD cohorts and applied disproportionately to schools with higher test scores. Thus "skimming" occurred at both the middle and high school levels—that is, some schools were drawing a disproportionate number of students from the high-scoring pool (in the case of certain schools, all of their students), whereas other schools were losing a disproportionate number of these students.

Skimming had its most demonstrable impact on middle schools.[3] In general, the students requesting open enrollment for sixth grade had higher scores on the fourth grade Colorado Student Assessment Program (CSAP), taken in the previous year, than students in BVSD overall. Furthermore, although many middle schools were holding their own in terms of the CSAP scores of students open-enrolling in, versus those open-enrolling out, several others were significantly gaining or losing. For example, in the 1998–99 open enrollment year (for enrollment in 1999–2000), Eastern open-enrolled only one student, but lost approximately 40 through open enrollment. (All school names are pseudonyms.) Seventy-four percent of the students lost by Eastern were "proficient or advanced" on the CSAP, slightly higher than the overall BVSD proficient or advanced rate of 70%. MLK open-enrolled 10 students and also lost approximately 40. The students it gained were at the districtwide rate of, 70% proficient or advanced; the students it lost, however, were well above it at 89% proficient or advanced. By contrast, Pinnacle open-enrolled 58 students with a proficient or advanced rate of 91%, also well above the BVSD rate. Because Pinnacle is a charter school, it lost no students through open enrollment. (Eastern and MLK, by the way, had the highest minority enrollments among BVSD middle schools, at 33% and 53%, most of whom were Latinos; Pinnacle had among the lowest minority enrollments, 11%, most of whom were Asians.)

The effect of this pattern of open enrollment gains and losses on subsequent test scores was stark. At 91%, Pinnacle had the highest proficient or advanced rate on seventh-grade CSAPs in the district. Eastern and MLK had the lowest, 53% and 29% respectively. The overall rate for seventh-grade CSAPs in BVSD was 73%.[4]

Stratification by Race and Income

Race/ethnicity was a prominent feature of open enrollment patterns, both regionally and with respect to individual schools. Students were leaving several regions that had higher percentages of minorities, located in the eastern and northern portions of the district, for regions with lower percentages, located in the southern and southeastern portions of the district. This migration was also from regions with lower enrollments relative to their capacities to regions with higher enrollments relative to their capacities. Furthermore, whites were leaving high-minority schools through open enrollment at a disproportionate rate. At MLK whites were leaving at a rate nearly double their proportion of the school's population.

The repetition of these patterns over recent years has led BVSD schools to become significantly more stratified with respect to race/ethnicity since the mid-1990s. If we place the schools in quintiles according to the percentage of white students enrolled, with the first quintile being the schools with the lowest percentage of white students and the fifth being those with the highest percentage, we find that the top four quintiles (or 80%) of BVSD elementary, middle, and K–8 schools have remained relatively stable in terms of racial makeup since 1994 (see Figure 1).[5] The second quintile closely tracks the percentage of white students in the district overall, at roughly 80%; the three highest quintiles (or 60%) have each consistently had a higher percentage of white students than the district overall.

By contrast, a significant change occurred in the first quintile (the 20% of schools with the lowest percentage of white students enrolled). The percentage of white students in those schools dropped precipitously, from a median of 68% in 1994 to 44% in 2000.

This pattern is explained much more by whites open enrolling out of BVSD schools than by minorities open enrolling in, for schools with the sharpest drops in white enrollment also tend to

FIGURE 1. Quintile Medians of Percentage of White Students in BVSD Elementary, Middle, and K–8 Schools, Fall 1994 to Fall 2000

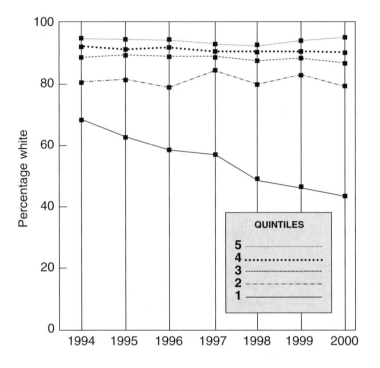

have sharp drops in enrollment overall. This pattern closely resembles one observed in New Zealand, where schools that were relatively high in minority enrollment saw an increase in their percentages of minority students when a choice system was implemented.[6]

Stratification of BVSD schools with respect to socioeconomic status has also increased since the mid-1990s, and the pattern is remarkably similar to that associated with race/ethnicity. Moreover, the association between socioeconomic status and minority enrollment, strong to begin with, became even stronger.[7]

Stratification by Special Needs

There was no discernible increase over time in stratification of special education students. But stratification no doubt exists beneath the radar of global statistics. For instance, there is evidence of stratification between "new mission" schools and other kinds of choice schools. In 2000–2001, three choice schools—a middle school emphasizing social responsibility, a high school emphasizing vocational education, and a high school serving adjudicated youth—had the highest percentages of special education students in the district (save for one school dedicated exclusively to students with severe disabilities): 23.3%, 25.9%, and 27.3% respectively, compared to 12.1% for the district overall.[8] At the other extreme, the three "new mission" schools most notorious for "elitism" had the three lowest special education percentages: 3.6%, 4.3%, and 5.4%.

Masked stratification is also quite likely with respect to BVSD's four Core Knowledge "strands" (schools within schools), for which only school-level data were available. The percentage of special education students enrolled by Colorado's Core Knowledge charter schools (the most popular kind by a wide margin) is roughly half that of the districts in which they are located.[9]

Stratification and Parent Motivation

The differences in demand for BVSD schools were more strongly associated with test scores and parental satisfaction ratings than they were with demographic makeup. Thus the leading explanation of stratification is that it is an unfortunate side effect of choice.

A significant group of Boulder critics eschews this explanation, contending that stratification among BVSD schools is evidence of "white flight" and is the direct result of racism, classism, and elitism. They believe that certain parents regard the demographic makeup of a school—the number of brown faces they see on a visit, for example, or the statistics reported in the newspaper—as a marker to determine its quality and whether it is the kind of school in which they would be comfortable enrolling their children.

Another explanation of the observed patterns is that parents get caught in the *draft* choice creates.[10] That is, they might not have thought much about the merits of school choice or might even be opposed to it, but they are motivated to participate out of the fear that, if they don't, their children will be the losers. We heard remarks in this vein from a number of participants in the Boulder study. Most dramatically, a distraught parent called one day and asked, "Have I made a mistake? Should I be open-enrolling my daughter in . . . ?" She was worried about the wisdom of keeping her child in her assigned neighborhood school in light of the fact that its enrollment and test scores were dropping while its proportions of minorities, students qualifying for free and reduced-price lunches, and students learning English as a second language were increasing. She was, by the way, a vociferous critic of the choice system.

Are BVSD parents motivated to choose schools by test scores and satisfaction ratings? By demographic characteristics? By fear? No doubt, each motivates some parents, singly or in combination. There are additional motivations as well, such as the proximity of schools to parents' workplaces. But whatever the motives driving individual parents, increased stratification is the undeniable outcome of their aggregated choices.

Stratification and Open-Enrollment Procedures and Practices

BVSD procedures and practices are potentially important factors in the patterns of stratification. First, the practice of prominently displaying test scores in the local newspaper's annual open-enrollment insert, as well as on district and school Web pages, helps explain the prominence of test scores in the demand for BVSD schools. Second, requiring parents to obtain their own information on open enrollment, providing most information in English only, requiring parents to visit schools in which they wish to open enroll their children, and requiring them to provide their own transportation help explain why choice has a stratifying effect. This system favors parents with savvy, time, and resources. It also favors parents who are connected to the parent information network, the importance of which was shown by how prominent word of mouth was as a student recruitment method.[11]

Certain schools (all charter or focus) give special enrollment preferences or set requirements that also contribute to stratification. These include 1) *legacies*, preferences afforded to certain groups, such as siblings of graduates, children of teachers, and staff members; 2) *ability to pay*, preferences for students previously enrolled in a tuition-based preschool program; 3) *screening*, additional application requirements, such as interviews and supplementary forms to fill out; and 4) *sweat equity contracts*, additional expectations for parental participation, formalized in written agreements.

In the case of special education, BVSD policy requires that a special-needs student must, after receiving "conditional acceptance" for enrollment at a school, "have a staffing which finds that the open enrollment placement is appropriate before a change in attendance can occur."[12] This policy provides a means of steering special-needs students away.[13] Once a student is flagged as having special needs, he or she may be denied enrollment via the staffing because of "lack of fit."

FUNDING AND FUND-RAISING

In distributing its general fund dollars, the Boulder Valley School District makes no special provisions for the proportion of low-income students in a school, despite the fact that the district receives an additional allocation for low-income students in accordance with the Colorado State Finance Act. Certain schools do receive additional money for low-income students through Federal Title I funding. In most qualifying schools, however, fewer than a third of low-income students are supported by Title I funds. BVSD also provides auxiliary funds to needier schools for dropout prevention and family resource centers, for instance. But such funds generally are not designated for core instructional programs or reductions in class size—the kinds of things that render schools attractive to many parents taking advantage of choice.

All BVSD schools generate additional funds in various ways, ranging from selling grocery store coupons, wrapping paper, and candy to soliciting parents to donate stocks. These fund-raising dollars are used to pay for library and classroom books, curriculum materials, computers, art supplies, physical education equipment, adjunct faculty, guest speakers, field trips, building improvements, staff development for teachers, and stipends for teachers to attend out-of-state professional meetings.

Because charter schools have wide discretion, they can use fund-raising dollars for additional purposes, such as increasing teacher salaries. And because charter schools do not fall under the normal budgeting processes of the district, they also have more discretion in the use of district funding. Thus the district funding that charter schools receive is like a voucher that they can supplement with fundraising, apparently without limit.

Our study found that, as a school's percentage of low income students increased, its ability to raise funds decreased, and vice versa. A low percentage of students qualifying for free and reduced-price lunches did not guarantee a high fund-raising amount, but those schools that raised the most had relatively low percentages of those students. On the other hand, high percentages of students qualifying for free and reduced-price lunches pretty much guaranteed low per-pupil fund-raising amounts. For example, the most successful of the elementary schools with a high percentage of students qualifying for free and reduced-price lunches raised $75 per pupil, whereas the most successful of the elementary schools with a low percentage of such students raised $278 per pupil.

IMPLICATIONS FOR THE BROADER SCHOOL CHOICE CONTROVERSY

We now return to the three general categories of controversy about school choice policy that we sketched early on, namely, competition, meeting student needs, and equity. We will compare the perceptions of BVSD parents and educators with what our other findings say—or can't say—about these matters.

Competition

Many BVSD parents and educators see competition as the driving force in obtaining district resources and support. To our knowledge, BVSD has never declared that competition will be the mechanism by which it decides the levels of support to be provided to its schools, but it has adopted this mechanism by default. The resources provided to BVSD schools (and, in the extreme, decisions about whether they will be closed or consolidated) are tied almost exclusively to enrollment, for which all schools must compete.[14]

Test scores loom large in how schools fare in the competition. Test scores are strongly associated with the open enrollment demand for BVSD schools, especially among middle-income whites. As these parents move to high scoring schools, which are already heavily populated by white middle-income students, they take their various resources with them and further stratify BVSD schools with respect to race/ethnicity and income, in addition to test scores. The schools they depart are left with fewer resources and larger percentages of low-income and minority students. These changes complicate their educational missions, both administratively and in the classroom. The result is a "spiral of decline" for schools losing enrollment: they have relatively low test scores; they lose parental resources; and, due to decreased enrollment, they begin to experience cuts in resources from the district. Their test scores drop further, they lose more parental resources, and so on. All along they scramble to find new programs to attract students, further complicating and intensifying their work.

Proponents of competition contend that it works to boost achievement overall, even if some schools may decline. This must be classified as conjecture in the case of BVSD. The fact that some BVSD choice schools, particularly "new mission" schools, have high—remarkably high—test scores does not prove that competition has stimulated increased achievement in BVSD schools overall. To confirm this claim would require longitudinal data spanning the mid-1990s, when choice burgeoned, and such data are not available.

The evidence that is available provides little reason to believe that an overall improvement in achievement has been an outcome of choice. On the contrary, it indicates that choice is more likely a zero-sum game with respect to achievement—a situation in which some schools do better only at the expense of others that do worse. There is suggestive evidence at the high school level and strong evidence at the middle school level that certain schools are disproportionately gaining high-scoring students and others are disproportionately losing them and that these gains and losses best explain the test scores that schools produced.

Focus and charter schools embraced competition, for the most part. This is consistent with the fact that these schools were born competing for students and with a commitment largely limited to their own programs. Moreover, competing for students has served them well. But a significant portion of BVSD's other schools— schools that have had to take on competing for enrollment as a new activity—perceive the competition for students as having mainly negative effects on them. Parents and educators in these schools see themselves as being required to divert time and resources away from curriculum and instruction and toward keeping their enrollments up, a demanding task that increases their total effort. They also believe that competition for students has engendered a breakdown of collegiality, as individual schools are forced to look after their own interests and to place them above those of the district as a whole.

Meeting Student Needs

By and large, BVSD parents are satisfied with the schools to which they send their children, and those who send their children to focus or charter schools are the most satisfied. This applies across BVSD's array of choice schools: to predominantly white, "new mission" schools, emphasizing academics; to largely Latino schools, emphasizing diversity and bilingualism; and to various kinds of alternative schools, emphasizing student participation or vocational education. Increased parental satisfaction is one of the claims made on behalf of school choice, and this is an apparent benefit of BVSD's choice system.

But this claim faces the same difficulty as the parallel claim about achievement. Parental satisfaction is a factor in judging the effects of choice on BVSD schools, but overall satisfaction is what should be at issue. If some parents are more satisfied only at the expense of others' being less so, then choice is a zero-sum game. Tackling this question, again, requires longitudinal data that span the period when open enrollment burgeoned, and again, such data are unavailable. Thus the claim that choice has resulted in an *overall* increase in parental satisfaction is also conjecture.

Significantly obscured by questions about how well needs are being met (as measured by parental satisfaction) is the prior question of how to think about and identify student needs in the first place. Traditionally, the focus has been on "special needs" that require additional resources, efforts, and methods to meet—for example, the needs of special education students, of those with limited proficiency in English, or of at-risk populations in general. But in BVSD (and elsewhere, to be sure), the idea of student needs has been stretched to include the need for a rigorous academic/college-preparatory education.

If a rigorous academic/college-preparatory education is a need, it is certainly of a different order from the needs described above. There is nothing special about it that warrants schools specifically devoted to it. Although there are differences among groups of

BVSD parents and educators on the question of how single-mindedly they can or should pursue the goal of increased academic achievement, each group places academic achievement at or near the top of the list of things that schools ought to accomplish. Culling academic achievement out as a special need that may be used to define the mission of certain BVSD schools has resulted in tracking writ large—tracking between schools rather than *within* them. And tracking brings with it racial/ethnic and income stratification.

The idea that schools should promote social/citizenship skills was also high on every group's list. But if social/citizenship skills include the ability to appreciate and interact with a diversity of people—and it is difficult to see how this could not be the case—then students who are separated off into homogeneous, predominantly white schools will not acquire essential skills. From this perspective, their education is impoverished.

Equity

One of the complaints frequently lodged against the choice system is that it is inequitable because it sets up unfair competition among BVSD schools. One solution is to level the playing field—for example, by permitting neighborhood schools to compete under the same set of rules as focus and charter schools. Although this would be an improvement, it implicitly concedes that competition is the principle that ought to determine which schools thrive and which are judged "good." (Test scores are currently the major determinant of both.) More fundamental concerns about the principle of competition exist, concerns grounded in equity.[15]

Letting things shake out through competition does not ensure equity because it does nothing to address the problem of the inequity experienced by students and educators languishing in schools caught in or threatened by the spiral of decline. Addressing this problem requires invoking another principle: ensuring that all students receive a good education, on equitable terms.

Letting things shake out through competition does not ensure equity even for those schools that manage to keep their enrollments up. Consider BVSD's bilingual schools. That Latino families are getting their choice of bilingual schools and that these schools are maintaining their enrollments does not mean that Latinos are getting the same kind of benefits as whites who are enrolling their children in homogeneous, high-achieving schools. Unlike the bilingual schools, which face a complex set of challenges, these high-achieving schools can be single-minded in their pursuit of achievement because they have a homogeneous set of students who predictably do well. Despite the relatively easier task they have to perform in comparison to bilingual schools, these schools get the same per-pupil funding from the district. They typically also have more additional resources at their disposal through fund-raising. Again, the uses to which such funds are put—books, computers, staff development, and, in some cases, teacher salaries—are anything but marginal to the quality of education that schools can provide.

In addition to the fact that there is inequality in the costs and benefits associated with the school choices that BVSD parents make, there is inequality in the opportunities for parents to choose at all. Lack of transportation, time, and information eliminate or diminish the opportunities of many parents to participate.

CONCLUSION: ON THE BUS FROM THE MOVIE *SPEED*

"We're on the bus from the movie *Speed*" is how one middle school principal described Boulder's open enrollment system, adding, "There's no mission, just more choices." Choice is "smoke and mirrors," he went on to say.

These remarks could just as aptly be applied to the national scene. The school choice bus continues to gain momentum and to pull politicians, policy makers, parents, and educators into its draft. This is so despite the fact that the research evidence is mixed at best, negative at worst. The research on vouchers, for example, has failed to show any but the most modest and equivocal gains for participating students.[17] The research on charter schools is increasingly showing that they encourage stratification by race, income, and special needs and that they fall short on the criterion of innovation.[18]

Not to oversimplify, the charter school movement—unlike vouchers—originally involved a strong commitment to what might be called an experimentalist rationale. The idea was that freeing a limited number of schools from bureaucratic rules would lead to experimentation and the improvement of public education overall. This rationale typically emphasized serving at-risk students, creating genuine innovations, and disseminating successful innovations to the larger public education system. But the experimentalist rationale always existed in tension with the market rationale underlying vouchers. As the market faithful wound up in the driver's seat, the various principles and restrictions associated with the experimentalist rationale went by the boards. Under the market rationale, the idea of *public education* has become indistinguishable from the idea of *publicly funded education*.

Given the effort and expense it would take to get school choice right—free transportation and concerted efforts to disseminate accessible information are minimum requirements—we would do well to abandon it as a failed school reform idea. At most, it should be viewed as but a relatively minor addition to the much more sweeping changes that are required. But it is probably too late to stop the bus. The best that can be hoped for now is to get it under better control.[19]

NOTES

1. Arizona, for instance, the state with the largest charter school movement by far, has a mere 4% of its students enrolled in charter schools. See *The State of Charter Schools 2000, Fourth-Year Report* (Washington, D.C.: U.S. Department of Education, 2000), available at http://www. ed.gov/pubs/charter4thyear/.

2. But see Casey P. Cobb and Gene V. Glass, "Ethnic Segregation in Arizona Charter Schools," *Educational Policy Analysis Archives* (January 1999); available at http://epaa.asu.edu/epaa/v7n1.

3. We were unable to investigate skimming in the elementary schools because we had no entering test data (the vast majority of open enrollment in elementary schools occurs at kindergarten). In the case of high schools, we lacked comparable test data. Also, because most high schools are relatively large, open-enrolled students constitute a relatively small proportion of the population, and, because we were limited to school level data, we could not tease out the special programs (or "tracks") into which they enroll.

4. This discussion is based on scores on reading tests, but the results were the same for writing.

5. This analysis excluded high schools for considerations similar to those discussed in note 3. The total number of elementary, middle, and K–8 schools fluctuated because of the opening of new schools and the closing or consolidation of others. There were 39 in 1994, 40 in 1995, 44 in 1996, 45 in 1997, 45 in 1998, 46 in 1999, and 47 in 2000.

6. Edward Fiske and Helen Ladd, *When Schools Compete: A Cautionary Tale* (Washington, D.C.: Brookings Institution, 2000).

7. Kenneth Howe and Margaret Eisenhart, "A Study of the Boulder Valley School District's Open Enrollment System," available at http://education.colorado.edu/EPIC (then click on the "Research and Publications" link).

8. Boulder Valley School District, "October Count," November 2000.

9. The 1998–99 Colorado Charter Schools Evaluation (Denver: Colorado Department of Education, 2000), available at http://www.cde.state.co.us/cdechart/download/ch99eall.pdf.

10. This kind of motivation has been documented in New Zealand. One official remarked, "Choice is like a neurosis . . . parents are motivated by fear. They feel that they have to look around to make sure they will not destroy their children's futures" (Fiske and Ladd, p. 183).

11. Howe and Eisenhart, op. cit.

12. This requirement is set forth on the district's website: http://www.bvsd.k12.co.us/eduprograms/bv_openenroll.html#special (accessed on 4 February 2001).

13. An analysis of the practice of steering special education students away from choice schools is developed more fully in Kevin Weiner and Kenneth Howe, "Steering Toward Separation: The Evidence and Implications of Special Education Students' Exclusion from Choice Schools," in Janelle Scott, ed., *School Choice and Diversity* (New York: Teachers College Press, forthcoming).

14. A controversial school consolidation involving five elementary schools was carried out for the 2000–2001 school year. One school with a high percentage of special education students and two schools with ESL programs, high percentages of students qualifying for free and reduced-price lunches, and high percentages of minority students were consolidated into one building and given a new name. The remaining two schools were focus schools with relatively few at-risk students. Each had previously shared a building with one of the three schools that was closed, and both moved into one of the buildings that had become available. Each retained its previous name, curriculum, student body, and separate identity.

15. Hugh Lauder and David Hughs, *Trading in Futures: Why Markets in Education Don't Work* (Philadelphia: Open University Press, 1999).

16. See, for example, Martin Carnoy, "School Choice? Or Is It Privatization?," *Educational Researcher* October 2000, pp. 15–20. See also the recent exchange in *Education Week* between Alex Molnar and Charles Achilles, "Voucher and Class-Size Reduction Research," 25 October 2000, p. 64; and William Howell et al., "In Defense of Our Voucher Research," 7 February 2001, pp. 32–33, 52.

17. As researchers have moved beyond large-scale surveys (e.g., *The State of Charter Schools* 2000) to more fine-grained analyses of individual states, the stratification by race, income, and special needs and the lack of innovation are being increasingly documented. See, for example, Amy Stuart Wells, *Beyond the Rhetoric of Charter School Reform: A Study of Ten California School Districts* (Los Angeles: University of California at Los Angeles, 1998); David Arsen, David Plank, and Gary Sykes, *School Choice Policies in Michigan: The Rules Matter* (East Lansing: Michigan State University, 2000); Kenneth Howe and Kevin Weiner, "The School Choice Movement: Déjà Vu for Children with Disabilities?" *Journal of Remedial and Special Education* (in press); and Cobb and Glass, op. cit.

18. The market rationale also won out in New Zealand. See Fiske and Ladd, op. cit.

19. In this vein, the Boulder Valley School District has taken the step of centralizing open enrollment to help mitigate the inequities. Moreover, fund raising is ongoing, and the district is considering the provision of free transportation and changes in funding.

Conclusion:
STEPS WE CAN TAKE

PATRICK SHANNON

Despite the scope and vigor of business activities in public schools, we believe that the principles of good education can prevail. Our hope stems from two sources. First, we take heart in the many questions posed by the authors in this book and the scores of others whom we could not accommodate. Those questions tug at the new practices of commercialism, market logic, and privatization that pervade our schools. Some of those questions are deeply troubling: "What happens to education for democracy when consumerism drives the curriculum?" Others are profoundly simple: "How can we talk about learning without the metaphor of work?" Each question opens spaces for us to consider the appearance of business practices in schools and to rethink the illusion that they are necessary and benign.

Second, we find hope in the openness of concern. Although the authors here suggest many points of entry in their analyses, they do not present ready-made solutions or heroes to direct our efforts. None seem ready to sell us a quick fix for business practices in and around schools. Too often when such solutions fail—and they must fail—they reinforce the illusion of necessity and foster cynicism and complacency. Rather the authors lay the responsibility for understanding and action before us all. They suggest that by asking their questions in local contexts and by posing questions of our own, we can uncover the essence of Education, Incorporated, and, perhaps, of public schooling itself. They do not promise complete victory, only the satisfaction of personal involvement in a cause that may yield small victories. These authors ask us to join them and to act on the new knowledge gained here.

In that hopeful spirit, we offer further sources for those who wish to form new questions and to act in coordination with others. We've collected resources for each of the sections of the book and added a fourth category for those who begin to see connections between business insurgencies in schools and similar activities in other parts of our public and private lives.

COMMERCIALISM IN SCHOOLS

The first four articles make the case that we are selling our children's attention to business. In return, our schools receive services and equipment. Pouring rights, hall advertisements, and force-fed commercials brand students with company logos, which often last a lifetime. Moreover, the content of free, corporate-sponsored curricula or the eight minutes of Channel One "news" presents a too-rosy picture of the role of business in everyday life without the opportunity for the complexities of that role to be considered. Phyllis Schlafly, Ralph Nader, even the federal government, agree that business has gone too far in these matters.

The seven websites that follow provide an opportunity to keep abreast of the latest business forays into schools. All suggest that many people are working to counteract this trend. The Kenway and Bullen book provides more depth on the psychological and social consequences of commercialism and young children.

Adbusters—*www.adbusters.org*
Center for the Analysis of Commercialism in Schools—
  www.schoolcommercialism.org
Center for Commercial-Free Education—
  www.commercialfree.org
Corporate Watch—*www.corpwatch.org*
Commercial Alert—*www.commercialalert.org*
The Center for a New American Dream—*www.newdream.org*
No Logo—*www.nologo.com*
Jane Kenway and Elizabeth Bullen—*Consuming Children: Education–Entertainment–Advertising.* New York: Open University, 2001.

MARKET LOGIC IN SCHOOLS

Behind much of the rhetoric about higher standards and school improvement lies the belief that the future will require that we all enter the marketplace as entrepreneurs able to move between jobs effortlessly according to where businesses might need us. This assumption creates enormous pressure on schools, teachers, and parents to find new ways to prepare our youth to enter that world. The middle six articles explain that business hopes to train our sensibilities to be more than just consumers of their goods. Many recognize that the bells between classes, the individual desks, and the compartmentalization of subject areas are designed to prepare most students for the world of work that awaits them. The authors of these articles recognize that the movement of high-stakes testing into elementary grades, metaphors of discipline, and emphases on developing human capital through lifelong learning (beginning in kindergarten) projects a sense of competition among individuals and a personal accountability for later success or failure.

We offer three sets of sources for those interested in pursuing the human and material consequences of market logic in schools. The first set provides overviews of neoliberalism—the animating philosophy of school and social reforms in the United States during the last decade, in which the market is to decide the value of all things. The second set presents information on school funding because the lack of public funds for schools drives them into the marketplace in order to obtain the goods and services that they identify as necessary. The final set is about how media represents the world to us through corporate eyes.

Overviews of Neoliberalism

Anne Birdsong, "The Claws and Teeth of Capitalist Neoliberalism"—*www.wam.umd.edu/~song/neoliberalism.htm*

"Bad Subjects: Political Education for Everyday Life"— *http://eserver.org/bs/*

Noam Chomsky, *Chomsky on Miseducation*. Landham, MD: Rowman & Littlefield, 2000.

School Funding

"Vermont Equitable School Funding"— *www.act60.org/index.html*

Bill Moyers on PBS, "Children in American Schools" (91367). Produced by South Carolina Educational TV (SCETV), 1996.

Media

"Kiss of the Panopticon"— *www.washington.edu/cmu/panop/home.htm*

Robert McChesney and John Nichols, *It's the Media Stupid*. New York: SevenStories Press, 2000.

PRIVATIZATION

The authors in the last section explain what we have to lose if we permit public schools to be sold to private business. Public schools were organized to be the backbone of democracy—institutions in which students of all classes, races, and religions would learn to understand and appreciate their differences and negotiate ways in which they could learn to live and work together with those differences. Although we have yet to approach this ideal, our struggle toward it makes the relationship between American public schooling and democratic self-government unique in the world. Because threats to democracy affect us all, we must commit ourselves to preserving and improving the public schools. We have many choices concerning the direction schools might take in a democracy, but privatization cannot be one of them.

> AFT Center for Privatization—*www.aft.org/privatization*
> Americans United for Separation of Church and State—*www.au.org*
> PBS Frontline, "Battle of School Choice"—*www.pbs.org/wgbh/pages/frontline/shows/vouchers*
> Economic Policy Institute—*www.epinet.org*
> Henry Giroux, *Stealing Innocence: Youth, Corporate Power, and the Politics of Culture*. New York: St. Martins Press, 2001.
> Deborah Meier, *Will Standards Save Public Education?* Boston: Beacon Press, 2000.
> NEA Voucher Resource Center—*www.nea.org/issues/vouchers/index.html*
> People for the American Way—*www.pfaw.org*
> Research for Action—*www.researchforaction.org/edisonarchive.html*
> Rethinking Schools—*www.rethinkingschools.org*

JOINING OTHERS TO ACT

Wearing a Coca-Cola shirt on Pepsi day, neglecting to write the jobs essay in elementary school, refusing to submit grants for instructional materials, or speaking out about the racist undertones of vouchers are individual acts of courage, any or all of which can register your concern over the current direction of schools in this country. Such acts open spaces for others to begin to ask questions about commercialism, market logic, and privatization. In those spaces, we meet others who share our concerns for the insurgence of business into schools and who extend that concern into the other problems schools face. Together we have a better chance of pushing beyond simply exposing the illusions of business generosity to affirm the essence of public schools. Each of the organizations in the following list has taken those first courageous steps in order to open spaces for discussion and action to challenge the current role of business in schools. These steps are part of larger projects that the organizations invite you to join.

> ERASE (Expose Racism to Advance School Excellence)— *www.erc.org/erase*
>
> GLSEN (Gay, Lesbian, and Straight Educators Network)— *www.glsen.org*
>
> National Coalition of Alternative Community Schools— *www.ncacs.org*
>
> National Coalition of Education Activists—*www.nceaonline.org*
>
> Power to the Youth—*http://youthpower.net*
>
> Rouge Forum—*www.pipeline.org/rgibson*
>
> Teachers for Democratic Culture—*www.tdc2000.org/home*
>
> Whole School Consortium—*www.coe.wayne.edu/ CommunityBuilding*

CONTRIBUTORS

Russ Baker is a New York journalist who covers politics and media.

Damian Betebenner is a post-doctoral fellow at the Education and Public Interest Center at the University of Colorado, Boulder.

Samuel Bowles is a professor of economics at the University of Massachusetts and an external faculty member at the Santa Fe Institute.

Karen Brandon writes for the *Chicago Sun-Times*.

Margaret Eisenhart is a professor of education and fellow at the Education and Public Interest Center at the University of Colorado, Boulder.

Sara Freedman, who has taught in urban classrooms and at Boston College, is now affiliated with the Boston-based Center for Collaborative Education.

Herbert Gintis is a professor of economics at the University of Massachusetts and the head of the Network on Norms and Preferences.

Henry A. Giroux is the Waterbury Chair in Secondary Education at The Pennsylvania State University and director of the Forum for Education and Cultural Studies.

Constance L. Hays is a columnist on business and industry for the *New York Times*.

Kenneth Howe is a professor of education and the director of the Education and Public Interest Center at the University of Colorado, Boulder.

Alfie Kohn is the author of eight books, and scores of articles, on education and human behavior. His most recent books include *The Schools Our Children Deserve* and *The Case Against Standardized Testing*. He lives (actually) in Belmont, MA, and (virtually) at www.alfiekohn.org.

Robert Lowe is a professor of education at the University of Wisconsin, Milwaukee and a member of the Rethinking Schools group.

Stephen Metcalf is a freelance writer living in New York City.

Barbara Miner was until recently the managing editor of *Rethinking Schools*.

Alex Molnar is a professor of education at Arizona State University where he directs the Commercialism in Education Research Unit.

John Olson is a professor of education at Queens University, Ontario, Canada.

Joseph A. Reaves is a professor of education at Arizona State University and the editor of publications for the Commercialism in Education Research Unit.

Patrick Shannon, a former preschool and primary grade teacher, is currently professor of education at The Pennsylvania State University. His books include *Reading Poverty*; *iSHOP, You Shop*; and *Becoming Political, Too*.

Makani N. Themba is a journalist based in Columbia, Maryland and a member of the editorial board for the Media Alliance.

INDEX